STRIKIN

STRIKING OUT

How to leave home and like it

Christine Brady

COLUMBUS BOOKS
LONDON

'This isn't a rehearsal. This is Life. Don't miss it.'

Copyright ©1984 Christine Brady

First published in Great Britain in 1984 by
Columbus Books
Devonshire House, 29 Elmfield Road, Bromley, Kent BR1 1LT

Jacket design by Astrid

Design and production in association with Book Production
Consultants, 47 Norfolk Street, Cambridge

Typeset by Cambridge Photosetting Services, 19–21 Sturton Street,
Cambridge

Printed and bound by Richard Clay PLC, Bungay, Suffolk

British Library Cataloguing in Publication Data
Brady, Christine
    Striking out
    1. Home economic
    I. Title
    640   TX145

ISBN 0 86287 166 2
ISBN 0 86287 099 2 Pbk

Note
Throughout this book the personal pronoun 'he' is often used as
a generic, for he *or* she: no sexual bias is intended.

The main body of the text does not contain addresses or phone
numbers. All these are listed, chapter for chapter, in the
reference section, together with other information that comple-
ments the ideas and suggestions made in the text.

Contents

CHAPTER 1

What it's all about

Deciding to leave home is a pretty big decision to take. It sounds fun not to have anyone to tell you what to do or get angry when you come in late. The idea of eating what you like and when you like and having all your friends round for an evening can be great once you have got somewhere to live and a job with regular money coming in. But unless you plan things carefully in advance it will not be like that at all.

Most people who leave home move to the big cities. Some go to college or university; others have heard that it is easy to get a job in London or Birmingham and they think that if they can just get there, then everything will fall into place. Unfortunately it is not that simple.

In big cities there is always a high demand for accommodation of any kind. The better flats and rooms are highly sought-after and landlords can afford to pick and choose their tenants. Jobs used to be easier to find in towns, but even this no longer applies. So it is essential to plan any move carefully and meticulously. The secret of success is in the planning.

If you go to college the decision about which town to go to will virtually be made for you, and you can then start to find out more about the area. If you just want to get away or go somewhere to find a better job or have more fun you can pick anywhere in the country, which makes the choice a lot more difficult.

For many people, the capital or one of the other big cities is the goal: somewhere exciting, stimulating, busy and offering plenty of opportunities for a good time. But having a good time comes after finding somewhere to live, getting a job and putting together a social life. The same applies to moving into any large town. It can work wonderfully well for you – or it can be a disaster

Try not to pick a place where you do not know anyone at all. Starting from scratch is difficult, but if you know someone you can drop in on when the going gets tough it can make a lot of difference.

So before you decide in which direction you are heading, find out if you have any connections in the town. Do your friends have addresses of people you could contact or do you have any relations, however distant, who could give you an anchor point? Make sure you review the job situation as well. Find out if there is high unemployment in the sort of work you want to do.

Exploring and settling into a new town is a lot more fun if you have someone with whom you can share the experience. Do you have a friend who would like to come with you? Even if the two of you do not stay together after you have found your feet you will still have a contact and an ally during the first few weeks.

Finding accommodation and getting a job will be discussed fully in Chapters 2 and 4, so work out your plan of action well before you fix a date to get up and go.

Even if you feel unhappy at home and long just to slam the door behind you and go – *don't*. Leaving home to strike out on your own takes a lot of planning if it is to be a success. So often girls and boys who leave home on the spur of the moment and go to the big city are penniless, homeless and back again within a few days. Drifting around without money or any idea of what to do next is a pretty scary way to start off what is going to be the rest of your life.

If you do not get on with your parents, you may be right to move out, but first find somewhere to live and try to discover what sort of a job you could get before you leave. Save up some money so that at least you can pay your fare and set yourself up in some basic accommodation. Find out if you could stay with a relative or at a friend's flat for a few days while you look around. London in particular sees floods of young people arrive in the capital with no job, no money and nowhere to go. The advice centres (see address list) do their best, but they cannot do anything more than offer very basic help and suggestions. Very often those who arrived with such high hopes are back home within a few days having lost what little confidence they had and feeling the world has rejected them. If they had taken time to plan and save it could have been a totally different story.

Sometimes the reason for leaving home is that the home leaves you. Parents may move house, uprooting a teenager just when he or she most needs to be with friends.

When this happens the practical solution might be to stay put where you feel you belong and either move in with a friend or become a lodger in the locality.

This can work well and will probably be less of an upheaval than moving to a different area where you do not know anyone and everything is very strange.

ADAPTING TO YOUR NEW ENVIRONMENT

Once you have decided to move, and decided on the general area, take time to get to know the neighbourhood. By far the best way to do this is on foot. Walk around the streets, buy a street map, find out what is special about the area – there might be a famous church or a museum to visit, or a good theatre or sports centre. Get to know the local shops, not just the big ones in the high street but the little stores in the backstreets and down alleyways. You will feel far more settled and in command of the situation once you know where to find things. Get to understand the local transport system, whether bus, train or Underground. Keep timetables handy and experiment in finding different ways to get to work.

When you first move to the city you may find you are full of tension because of the noise, the dirt and the endless crowds. This is a perfectly normal reaction if you have come from a small town or village. The lack of personal space may worry you – the fact that you seem to have to queue for everything from getting on a bus to being served in the shops.

Eventually this feeling will pass; although you may still find it worrying, you will get used to it and find it less stressful. You will also learn your own way of adapting to it: a visit to the park for an early-morning jog before too many people are up and about; or shopping first thing in the morning, which usually means fewer customers and an opportunity to move around quickly. Travelling in off-peak times is fine if you can arrange your timetable accordingly. You will even learn a way to walk through crowds without feeling hassled.

PARENTAL TIES AND INDEPENDENCE

It is a traumatic moment, especially for a mother, when children break the ties that have bound them for anything up to twenty years. When you are getting older, especially if you have spent all your time looking after a family, it creates a great void when your offspring leave home. That is why mothers often find it difficult to let go, because they are frightened of what will happen to them in the future and that they will end up unwanted. It can happen with fathers, too. So if your mother makes a fuss or even resorts to tears, do not get too upset or overreact. It is all quite natural. If your parents can come to terms with the fact that you have gone but that you will be coming back to visit it will certainly make life smoother for you and happier for them.

For a start, going back home to visit will usually ensure you get one or two good, substantial meals – very important if you are living on a small budget. You might sometimes bring your washing home or borrow money. So from a practical point of view it is sensible to stay friends with your parents. From an emotional point of view, too, it can help enormously. Provided you have had a fairly normal relationship with your mother she is one of the few people in your life who will defend you whole-heartedly against the rest of the world whether you are right or wrong. That is worth hanging on to.

Many parents and children find at this stage that they grow closer than ever. The relationship changes, in subtle ways, so that they meet more and more on equal terms. The younger people's opinions and ideas breathe new life into the older generation of the family and parents listen to their sons and daughters, perhaps for the first time, with interest and consideration.

For most sons and daughters, living at home has meant that they have had someone to look after them: to nag them about going to the dentist, take care of them when they have the 'flu or collect them from parties if they miss out on transport home.

Being on your own will soon teach you that you have to stand up for yourself. Standing on your own two feet, dealing with problems without resorting to Dad or Mum or big brother, will give you a sense of achievement – after it is all over, if not at the time! Dealing with a flat tyre, being locked out of the flat, having your wallet stolen or fusing the lights will soon teach you that it is necessary to learn basic practicalities if you are to live a happy life without being propped up by a background army.

You will learn to develop your own sixth sense about people and situations, and on the whole it is as well to follow your instincts. If you feel something is wrong, either about your job or in a relationship, even if you cannot describe what it is, deep down you are probably right.

We all send out signals – in the way we talk, dress, walk and even the way we fold our arms. So even if you do not know it, you are responding to what psychologists call 'body language'. It is a fascinating subject in itself, on which books have been written, but as you go out and about and meet more people from different backgrounds and cultures you are unknowingly sifting and storing experiences and filing them in your subconscious for future use.

EXPECTATIONS AND SELF-KNOWLEDGE
Once you have set yourself up as an independent operator, do not expect life to be one long, smooth path. Life has a way of

playing tricks and just as you feel you are in control, you are jolted. Some days you will feel on top of the world for no particular reason. It may just be that the sun is shining, you have had a phone call from someone you care about or you enjoyed the film the night before. But at other times, for far less obvious reasons, you will feel depressed and wonder whether you can really work things out. The main thing is to stick with it. Both good and bad feelings pass eventually. Everyone has peaks and troughs in their lives and has to learn to adjust day by day.

If you find that your life is one long disaster area you should consider very carefully whether it is of your own making. We all make mistakes, but if you go on running out of money, being asked to move out of your flat or being overlooked at promotion time, it is prudent to analyse why. It could be that you are in the wrong life stream. Perhaps you have not assessed your own potential and style correctly. Many people tend to underrate themselves and do not stretch themselves sufficiently, but there are others who find that they have been pressurized by other people's expectations of them to overreach and go into a job or lifestyle that is unappealing or beyond their capabilities. We all know of stories of sons or daughters pushed into their parents' careers when really they would have been far happier in a totally different environment.

It is not only parents who influence our choice of lifestyle and even careers. It can be teachers, friends or brothers and sisters. There are 'high-achiever' families in which everyone appears to excel, but sometimes one member of the family endures much pressure and stress in the struggle to keep up.

However well you have planned, do not expect to feel completely at ease and happy right away. Cutting off parental ties, moving to a different area, leaving friends behind and dealing with a new set of situations are all dramatic experiences. So if you feel a sense of panic, or maybe homesick, do not worry; it will pass. On the days you do feel low, try to have a plan of action that you know will give you a lift. 'Phone Home' didn't just apply to E.T.: you will get a moral boost if you phone your parents, brother or sister for a chat, buy a record, see a film – or do whatever you regard as a treat.

ALONE, NOT LONELY
Learning to be on your own and like it is one of the most important life skills you can learn. If the future follows current trends, more and more of us will spend a certain amount of time in our lives living on our own, so it is important to know how to cope.

One thing is certain: at various stages we will be uncommitted to anyone else. In our teens most of us are enjoying ourselves hugely but also looking out for a life partner. This magical person we may or may not find. And when we do, it is only prudent to acknowledge that such an intimate personal relationship may not last.

We all know the sort of people who panic if they have not got someone to go out with or have to face a weekend when their friends are away or their husband or wife is working. Imagine the same person divorced or suddenly bereaved, and you can see that there is a major problem looming.

People who can accept that being alone can be good, if tackled in the right way, lead much happier and more fulfilling lives.

Teenagers who have had to share a room with a brother or sister and had nowhere to do their homework may long for privacy. So do busy mums when the toddler is banging on the bathroom door, making even a wallow in the bath a near-unattainable luxury. Although they may long for privacy, because they have had so little of it, the novelty of being completely alone soon wears off, to the extent that if they have half a day on their own they begin to feel lost. This is quite natural, and no one would argue that being alone does not feel strange to begin with. Accepting that it happens to all of us and that we can cope and learn to enjoy it makes it work for us positively. Being alone gives us time to pamper ourselves and be selfish, and there is nothing wrong in being selfish from time to time as long as it is not carried to extremes or hurtful to other people. Having time on our own to recharge the batteries can make us more able to cope with other human beings and deal with problems.

One of the secrets is to learn to take preventive measures on the days when we are likely to feel depressed. Some people find that it is Saturdays when they feel most lonely because most families have a busy day shopping. If that applies to you, make Saturday the day you treat yourself and do something you really enjoy, whether it is taking a trip to the seaside, window-shopping or going for a swim. Cultivate a network of friends to drop in on or telephone. Join local associations that do something positive, such as helping the community (see Chapter 12).

All these experiences contribute to growing up and maturing. The best thing about all of them, whether good or bad, is that we learn from them; it is when we go on making the same mistakes again and again that we should begin to worry.

Accepting that some mistakes or misjudgements are

inevitable, it is important not to keep harping back and dwelling on what went wrong. A certain amount of soul-searching is good, but if you are still agonizing over the occurrence months or even years after, there is something wrong. Having made the error you should have put it right, or learned to accept it and then moved on to other experiences.

Learning to understand yourself and be at ease in your own company is a necessary part of growing up and becoming a more confident human being. If you like yourself, there is every chance that other people will like you too.

It is important that you can cope with all of your life, whether it is eating out on your own, paying the bills, filling in a tax form or falling in and out of love without too much unhappiness. Learning to manage on your own is a matter of pride and of having faith in yourself. Then, when you do commit yourself to a close relationship, you can still be your own person and not lose identity. If you do not make that commitment you can still feel happy and fulfilled. In discovering and maintaining your own style and personality you will also become a more attractive and interesting person in your own right.

CHAPTER 2

Finding somewhere to live

However much you may long to leave home, remember that if you are under 16 the authorities will send you back home, or put you 'in care', because you may not legally leave home until you are 16. At 16 you can leave home with a parent's consent. At 18 you can go whether or not your parents agree.

It is not really a good idea to leave home the moment you are 16 unless you are doing so for the purposes of work or study. If you leave home for other reasons it is essential that you arrange somewhere suitable to live – perhaps with the parents of a friend, or with a relative, as you will find it very difficult to fend for yourself without more experience of life. Assuming that you have a good home to stay in and that you are not living with a boyfriend or in what might be termed 'unsuitable accommodation', and that you do not get yourself into trouble, you should not have too many problems – but you must still think the whole enterprise through.

Getting a roof over your head is one of the first and most important things to arrange when you are planning to leave home. If you are moving from one town to another, especially if you are planning to go to London, you may have to go there first and find a place to live once you are there. This means you will be spending precious savings on hostel or bed-and-breakfast accommodation while you look for something more permanent.

If you or your family have any friends in the area where you are planning to go, write or phone and ask them if they know anyone who can put you up for a few days while you get yourself organized. Failing that, write to a hostel or a bed-and-breakfast address to book a room before you set off.

The YMCA and YWCA provide accommodation for young people in various cities throughout Britain, and much of their work is focused in London.

The accommodation they provide is mostly self-catering and varies from single, double and shared bedsitting rooms to those where several people share kitchen facilities and a bathroom. Some hostels provide catering. Although some provide overnight accommodation, the hostels' main purpose is to provide longer-stay accommodation for people making the transition from living at home to full independence.

Rooms are very highly sought-after, so there is a long waiting-list for most hostels. Write well in advance to find out more about the hostel that interests you and to find out how long you may have to wait to get a place.

Not all hostels are as attractive as the YMCA/YWCA ones. Some of the cheapest hostels are not very smart and you may have to sleep in a dormitory. The bathroom and toilet facilities may have to serve a lot of people. Fellow guests may not have the same standards of cleanliness as you.

Cheap bed-and-breakfast addresses are often rather inadequate as far as facilities are concerned, but they could provide you with a stop-gap.

If you arrive in London or a large provincial city without having sorted out a place to stay you will need help. In London there are various organizations that help people in this situation and point them in the direction of beds for the night. They will also provide valuable advice on other matters, but it is far, far better to have found yourself a place to live in advance than to rely on the emergency accommodation that the staff of these centres will be able to suggest.

If you arrive with no money at all you may be given a bed in a free hostel for a few nights – but you will get a shock when you see what is on offer: you will sleep in a dormitory with up to 70 others, you will have no privacy and nowhere to store belongings – which could be stolen while you are asleep. None the less, such a hostel is considerably better than roaming the streets all night.

However you start off, your object will be to find a flat or a bedsitter, either on your own or sharing with others, where you can put some roots down and get on with enjoying the rest of your life.

You will probably decide before long that you like one part of the city better than another, so it is best to pinpoint a fairly small area and concentrate on that. It will save you time, and once you get to know the layout you will come to recognize from the map which place is opposite the park and which faces the gasworks.

Accommodation agencies exist in most large towns, but will probably charge for finding you somewhere to live. (It is illegal for an agency to make a charge just for registering a person's details or supplying addresses.) They may ask you to sign an agreement to pay something if and when they find you something suitable. As long as no money exchanges hands until you are fixed up, this is lawful.

Most agencies will ask for references. Be very wary of signing any agreement and make sure you understand it fully before putting pen to paper. If in doubt get expert help. Your local Citizens' Advice Bureau, or your local Law Centre if there is one, should be able to help you.

If you are flat-hunting in London, Capital Radio publishes a list twice a week on Tuesdays and Fridays. The list can be picked up after 11 am in the foyer of their building in Euston Road (opposite Warren Street tube station). Once again, be ready with a pile of coins so that you can make phone calls immediately.

If you are a student, a nurse or a medical student, your college or the hospital may be able to help you. Contact the Students' Union or the Bursar to find out what they can do for you.

Very often private landlords prefer to contact universities or hospitals when they are looking for new tenants because they feel this guarantees to some extent the sort of person who will be introduced, and that at least they will have some kind of comeback if the rent is not paid or if anything goes wrong.

You may hear of a bedsit or flat-share from a friend, or someone at work or at college, so it is worth putting the word about that you are on the lookout.

You may see an advertisement on a newagent's board. It is always worth investigating these. Look around the area that you have decided on; it might well be worth putting you own ad on the board. In this case you will have to 'sell yourself' so that whoever is reading the ad will decide that you will make a better tenant than anyone else. They will be looking for someone who can give a reference either from a previous landlord or a teacher or an employer. They will want to know that you can pay the rent promptly, have a stable form of income, whether from a job or a grant, and that you will be a quiet and pleasant person to have in the house. So an advertisement extolling your virtues may produce good results. In any case, cards in newsagents' windows are a cheap way of advertising and you will not have lost much if nothing comes of it.

If you work in a large firm you may be allowed to put a notice on the bulletin board. Ask your personnel department and enquire at the same time whether they know of anyone who wants to let a room.

Otherwise, you will probably find your best bet is the local paper. Be ready and waiting to buy it the minute it comes on sale. Do not waste time thinking you can go through the ads at the weekend or the following evening. Speed is vital, as a good flat or room will not be available for long.

Have plenty of coins ready for the phone-box and make

immediate contact with anyone offering a flat or room you think might suit you. Be polite and business-like on the phone. The landlord will be making up his mind who is going to get the flat or room from the moment he hears your voice. Make an appointment to view and keep the appointment.

Try to view the room immediately, and be ready to put down a deposit if you like it. You cannot afford to say, 'I'll think about it and let you know.'

Although finding a flat is a sellers' market, you should still be prepared to ask pertinent questions; and do not let an over-talkative landlord put you off having a good, hard look at what is on offer.

Are the rooms clean and cheerful-looking? Can you bring any of your own furniture? What are the arrangements for paying for heating and light? Are there any restrictions on, for example, taking baths or having visitors?

When you inspect a flat take a careful look at the electrical sockets – not only how many there are in each room, but the state of them as well. If the sockets have round holes they are very old, may be dangerous and will not fit any of the plugs on your appliances. Modern sockets have 'square' holes. If the sockets hang out of the wall, they are unsafe and you should insist they are attended to before you take over the flat.

You will probably find that the number of sockets is very limited, which can be extraordinarily frustrating. If you use two- or three-way adaptors you may find you have overloaded the system, and a fuse may blow. If you do not, you may find you cannot watch the television while using the electric heater.

If you are after a flat-share arrangement, find out how the chores are divided up and how the housekeeping works. How do the existing flat-sharers pay for basic foods like milk and tea, and is the TV rental shared equally?

Sharing a flat is usually cheaper than taking a bedsitter on your own, and provides an important link with other people – a great help if you are moving to a new area. They will be your substitute family, at least until you get a job and start making new friends. So it is important to like them and feel you will be able to get on. Trust your gut reactions and if you are doubtful whether you will fit in, grit your teeth and go on hunting.

Mixed flats have become popular during the last few years, and provided everyone is reasonably level-headed it seems to work quite well. Contrary to what the folks back home might think, mixed flat-sharing is not a license to hop in and out of bed with your flat-mates – rather the reverse.

Very often it is easier to allocate chores in mixed flats –

cleaning in exchange for going to the launderette, shopping in exchange for cooking. Girls may feel more secure from prowlers or peeping toms in the knowledge that there is a man in the flat. Although girls today can tackle most of the traditionally 'male' jobs, such as fixing a plug or decorating, and many boys are excellent cooks, and are handy with a sewing needle, there are times when a little brute force – or feminine flair – is very useful.

Landlords will almost certainly want not only a month's rent in advance but also a returnable deposit against breakages or damage (or you doing a moonlight flit without paying the rent). The deposit should be no more than two months' rent, and should be reasonable in relation to the facilities on offer. Find out exactly what it covers: fair wear and tear, for example, should be excluded. Get a receipt for any money you pay.

Most people prefer to take a flat where the landlord is not on the premises. It seems to give you more freedom as long as you pay the rent promptly. At least it prevents the owner constantly checking up to see what you are doing. If you do have your landlord on the premises it is important from both your points of view to try to get on well. This is easier if you are within a similar age bracket, as there is little doubt that older people tend to make fussy landlords, but of course there are always exceptions to any rule.

Good manners and consideration on both sides make for harmony. If you are having friends to stay it is better if the landlord knows so that he does not think he has burglars. Record-players blaring late at night are likely to annoy even the sunniest-natured person, whether landlord or neighbour, especially if he or she has young children or has to get up early the next morning. And it is to the landlord that neighbours will complain rather than you, the tenant.

All the foregoing advice might make you wonder if finding your own place is really worth the effort and expense. It will be, but be prepared for a fair amount of setbacks and disappointments before you achieve what you want: few people manage to find ideal accommodation the first time round – and if you are unlucky it can take a considerable while to find something reasonable, as the following true story shows.

Nik was never happy after his parents moved from one south London suburb to another. He spent all his time in his previous haunts, often missing the last bus or tube home and having to walk miles.

He used to stay with friends when he could, but often ended up sleeping in his car, which had broken down. This habit was eventually to lose him his job.

From sleeping in a car he went on to squatting with friends. Then he found a flat that was ridiculously cheap, in return for babysitting, but that did not last for long. He ended up sharing a flat with several friends, and that worked well for several years, although they moved around a lot. Nik always stuck out to have his own bedroom so that he could get away from everyone when the need arose. Then the landlord wanted to sell the house and he and his friends were offered a pay-off to move out. This gave Nik the basis for a deposit to buy a flat of his own. He borrowed the remainder of the deposit, took a mortgage and managed to buy a two-bedroomed flat, in the area where most of his friends still live.

Now he has his own flat, Nik lets a room to a friend who travels a lot, and the rent helps with expenses.

Nik's advice is to make sure you can always pay the rent or mortgage – it makes for a more peaceful life. Make a friend of the milkman and always pay the bill regularly, so that if you run out of cash mid-week you can always order bread, eggs and cheese from the roundsman to keep you in food until next payday.

ALTERNATIVE ACCOMMODATION

A less obvious possibility for accommodation is 'short-life housing'. Councils usually have empty property awaiting redevelopment and sometimes they are willing to let these properties to groups of people until the work starts.

The properties are usually in bad repair, so you either have to put up with this or join together to do something about it. The time the property stays available varies greatly, but sometimes it can be for a considerable period. In London, find out more about this type of housing from the Housing Advice Switchboard or SHAC; outside London contact the local council or a housing advice centre.

As a last resort, not to be recommended, there is squatting. Squatting itself is not illegal, but the way you do it may be, so you stand a risk of being prosecuted. If you are considering squatting contact the Advisory Service for Squatters, which publishes a book outlining squatters' rights and the procedures involved.

If you are looking for a 'gay' flat-share, try the accommodation service run by Gay Switchboard.

SECURITY AND INSURANCE

It makes sense to have your possessions covered by insurance as soon as you move into a flat. People coming and going at all times, many of whom will be comparative strangers, and possibly insecure locks, will make you vulnerable to burglary. Take out an insurance policy and make sure it covers any special items such as cameras, television sets, hi-fi and jewellery. Do not forget that the insurance company in turn will expect you to have secure locks on your door. Be sensible about the number of door keys you have in circulation and be careful not to leave windows open when you are out.

When you are all out make a special check that all doors and windows are securely locked. If you are all out at night leave a light on in a downstairs room rather than in the hall. Do not leave spare keys in 'safe' places: a burglar knows them all. Do not keep cash in the house.

It is possible to mark valuable items. You can use a security marker pen that contains invisible ink and is only visible under ultra-violet light. You can buy these in some stationers. Your name and postcode will be sufficient, in the event of theft, for recovered goods to be returned to you in future.

TENANTS' RIGHTS

If your landlord lives on the premises you will be renting the rooms under what is called a restricted contract. This means that if the landlord asks you to leave you will have to go, but there is a particular procedure that must be followed.

If the landlord has granted you the tenancy by the week or the month, with no final date stipulated, you have what is called a periodic tenancy. If he wants you to leave he must give you at least four weeks' notice in writing in the form required by law.

If you have nowhere to go, or just do not want to leave, you cannot be forced to go. Harassment or bullying by the landlord (say, by switching off the gas or electricity) is against the law. The landlord must obtain a court order to evict you. Such applications come before the courts fairly quickly, but the court may give you up to three months' security of tenure. They cannot give you any longer: after that you must go. However, if you stop paying the rent or any other agreed costs, such as rates, the landlord can go back to the court and possibly repossess the premises earlier.

If the tenancy was for a fixed period, the landlord is not required to give you any notice.

Very often a flat or bedsitter has a registered rent, which means the rent has been fixed by a rent tribunal. All the registered rents are shown on a register which you can see during normal working hours at the local rent-assessment panel's offices. Once this rent has been agreed it cannot normally be altered until two years have elapsed, or there has been a substantial change in the amenities provided, such as the installation of an extra bathroom or central heating.

If you have rented a flat and think the rent is too high you can apply to the rent tribunal for an assessment. The rent tribunal will speak to both you and the landlord before fixing the rent, and although it is unlikely you could run the risk of having the rent *raised* by the tribunal instead of lowered. The rent stays registered even after a tenant has left so if you are taking over a new tenancy the rent will still be as before.

If you are paying the rent weekly you should be provided with a rent book, unless a substantial amount of your rent is for meals supplied by the landlord. If you do not have a rent book you must have a receipt for money handed over as cash. Alternatively, pay by cheque or postal order and keep the stubs, or your bank statements, so that you can prove you have paid.

If you are worried about any aspect of your tenancy, go and see your local Housing Aid Centre or the Citizens' Advice Bureau.

BECOMING A LANDLORD

Julie found that when she rented a company flat she was not only poor, but lonely as well. At 23 years of age, she had had several years' experience of sharing flats and enjoyed the company. Then she thought, 'If I'm going to be poor in rented accommodation, why not be poor in my own flat instead?'

She looked around and decided she could just afford a studio flat if she could get a mortgage; but a studio flat would not provide her with an extra bedroom to have someone to share. She talked it over with her parents and found they were all for the idea of her buying a small house. Further investigation revealed that a three-bedroomed house was not much more expensive than one with just two bedrooms, so this is what she opted for, with a bit of help from her father.

She now has a pleasant three-bedroomed house of her own with two lodgers who help to pay the mortgage. Both her lodgers are friends so she charges them a little less than the going rate because she appreciates having people who are known to her as tenants, and because they all get on so well. Because they happen to be men, they appreciate the fact that she keeps the kitchen and bathroom clean, and she does not mind too much because it is her house.

Not everyone finds being a landlady so pleasant. Rowena took on the tenancy of a large London flat but found that constantly finding new flatmates, arguing about the phone bill, being held responsible for the rent and having to persuade people to pay up was more than she could manage, so she became ill. Because of gaps between tenants, when she was left to find the extra rent, she also got into financial difficulties, and an unpleasant tenant who caused trouble with the others was the last straw. She gave up the tenancy and went home to her mother.

Before you take on a tenancy which makes it necessary to find people to share, work out carefully what you need to cover yourself for the odd weeks when the house or flat is not full, and charge for the rooms accordingly. Take great care in choosing flatmates, and try to talk to people who have previously shared flats with them, if you can, to find out any hidden snags. Finding someone through friends is probably the best way to get someone, though if you fall out with your new tenant, you run the risk of falling out with the friend who recommended him or her too.

CHAPTER 3

Getting your place together

Very few furnished rooms or flats are sufficiently well furnished not to need a little smartening up. Some are so unattractively filled with old, dilapidated furniture that you may long to put it all to one side so that you can start again.

If you have the mind and the space to shut it away in one room or at least a corner, that is fine, but old and battered though it may be the furniture is not your property, and if you damage it more than it has been damaged already you may lose some or all of your deposit when you go.

Most new tenants make the best of what is available as far as larger items such as beds, tables and wardrobes are concerned, but they can be prettied up with a bit of ingenuity and a little spare time.

Remember you will probably move around quite a bit at first, so any items of your own that you acquire should be extremely portable and easy to remove.

TAKING STOCK

When you first get your room have a good, close look at the furniture you have inherited. Check that the bed is clean and the mattress in good condition. If it does not have one it is worth investing a few pounds to buy your own mattress cover. You might like to have your own fitted sheet and duvet set too: perhaps you could ask for one as a birthday present, for example. Choose the best you can afford as they last for a very long time and can easily move around with you from flat to flat.

If the bed sags, ask the landlord whether he could supply a board to go between base and mattress. If not, consider getting one yourself, especially if you suffer from back trouble. A good night's sleep is absolutely essential to everyone, and it is worth spending any money necessary to see that you are comfortable in bed.

Chairs and sofas that are sound but threadbare can be transformed if you drape colourful blankets, or even a large shawl, over them. Tuck in well between the seat and back and anchor with tightly rolled newspaper. A thick cloth over a badly marked table will make the room look more cheerful too.

If lack of seating is the problem, you can make giant-sized cushions very easily. (You can even make them from a good-quality sack.) Enterprising people fill them with their winter clothes in the summer and *vice versa* in the winter. It saves storage space and makes for a firm filling.

Rugs begged from friends or parents can hide a lot too. Use one or two bright rugs either to hide a frayed carpet or somewhere where they will look cheerful, but avoid areas where anyone is likely to trip.

The problem with a lot of furnished accommodation is that there are too many patterns jostling for position (on curtains, carpets and upholstery, for example) and nothing has ever been planned to match. Make sure you do not add to the visual chaos by adding yet more clashing tones or patterns.

Storage can often be a problem, too. One wardrobe may not cope with all your clothes and shoes and paraphernalia such as cameras, records and books.

Stout cardboard boxes, usually available free at supermarkets, can be transformed very cheaply with wrapping-paper. A cheaper way still would be to buy a roll of wallpaper and use that to cover them. A few bricks and wooden planks can make an excellent bookshelf. Tea-chests are sometimes on sale for £1 or so and are sturdy enough to make bedside or coffee tables. Because they are longer-lasting it may be worth while to cover them with self-adhesive plastic or hessian, or just with a pretty square of fabric.

Delivery trays are sometimes available and often stack together. They make excellent receptacles for clothes if they are stored under the bed or at the bottom of a wardrobe.

Lighting makes the world of difference to any room and can disguise a multitude of sins. The single overhead light casts an unkind glow on even the most lavishly furnished room – even more noticeable if the furnishings look rather tired. One or two strategically placed lamps can hide what needs to be hidden and throw light where you want it. Spotlights or more decorative lighting can be bought inexpensively from chain stores. Do not economize or do without lighting where it is needed for safety reasons. Keep a good light on the stairs and in the kitchen in particular.

The wiring in your new home may not be very up to date, so do not overload electrical sockets. You could even forget electricity on some occasions and use a paraffin lamp instead – either one of the reproduction Victorian ones or the type used on ships or for camping. If you keep paraffin in the home, do observe all the normal safety precautions, and check first that your landlord does allow paraffin to be kept in the house.

Such a ban may also apply to paraffin heaters, so check with the landlord first before you acquire one; keep paraffin in a proper, clearly marked container, outside the house if possible.

Life is certainly easier if you can assemble a few basic kitchen essentials that you can use comfortably and take with you from place to place. A good-quality frying-pan that does not stick and a couple of saucepans will make a good start, plus one or two sharp kitchen knives. A bread knife that really cuts will help to make you more efficient when you are cooking.

A couple of attractive mugs or cups and saucers that you enjoy drinking from can be a good investment too. They can be bone china bought in a sale or thick, chunky pottery bought from a craft shop. Buying one or two things that you enjoy using will give you inspiration later on when you are furnishing a proper place of your own from scratch.

If you run out of wardrobe space you can buy a portable plastic-covered one (available from many department stores), or you can use a plastic clothes-horse for hanging shorter items like skirts or blouses, and tuck it in a corner. If you have a picture rail that looks sufficiently strong you can make extra hanging space by linking dowel rods (from a DIY shop) strung together with nylon rope, like a rope ladder, with a clothes-hanger hook screwed into the top.

For the kitchen buy jams and pickles with an eye to the empty jars as they will stand you in good stead as containers to begin with. A set of labels can be bought from any stationers.

Plants can work wonders in cheering up a flat – rented or otherwise. It is amazing what something green and living can do to make a place look homely. Cut flowers are lovely, too, but frankly expensive, whereas a plant, with care and a certain amount of luck, can last for months or even years.

When you come to furnish a place of your own, you will want to see that what you buy is longer-lasting and you will have a different sense of priorities. Good-quality furniture is expensive and you are almost certain to have to go slowly. Meanwhile, make do with cheaper, more temporary, alternatives.

Many books have been written on cheap furnishings which are not only fun to read but have ideas in them which are a pleasure to try out.

Buying second-hand is fun, and as long as you have the time to go ferreting around you can save pounds. Newspaper ads and newsagents' boards are a good source of cheap three-piece suites, second-hand refrigerators and so on.

Classified ads should state whether the advertiser is a trader or not: this is important because of the law relating to the purchase of second-hand goods. If you buy from a trader you are protected by the Sale of Goods Act (see page 134). When buying from a private individual you do not have the same sort of protection, but the goods should be 'as described', so that if you buy a cooker said to be in working order and you find when you get it home that it is not, you are entitled to redress.

Skips in the streets can sometimes yield surprising finds, but do not think that because something is in a skip it is abandoned and you can therefore help yourself. You should ask the hirer of the skip whether you can take anything away. Sometimes skips are used to gather together items which will later be sold to a dealer, so you could be in trouble if you just take items you fancy.

Jumble sales are a good source of furniture as well as smaller items like saucepans, kettles and so on. Once again you need to have the time to search them out and get there early enough to join the queue before the doors open. A pair of sharp elbows helps too.

Floor-covering is always expensive, and unless the previous owners have left carpets intact you are in for a very expensive purchase.

Look for second-hand carpets in advertisements or buy hard-wearing coconut matting, which is practical but a little tough on bare feet. Some carpet tiles are inexpensive, too, and very easy to take with you when you move on. Rush matting is also inexpensive, and as all the dirt falls through to the floor you can lift it up and sweep the dust away quite easily.

Sanding and varnishing floors is a cheap way out of the problem of the floor. You can hire a sander for a day from a local hire shop, but wear a mask or the dust may choke you. Read as much as you can about the art of sanding floorboards before you start and be prepared to seal the boards with varnish immediately before they get stained or scuffed.

Some ambitious people paint patterned borders around the edge of the floor. It can look very attractive if you plan it properly and give the pattern several coats of varnish to protect it.

Emulsion paint is probably the cheapest way of covering the walls, with the added advantage that it does not take ages to prepare if you want to change the colour or brighten it up later on. But wallpaper will hide minor cracks and bumps and may look better in the long run. There are some inexpensive, highly attractive patterns available so look around.

Blinds are easy to make and take less fabric than curtains, although they are not so draught-proof, so if you get howling gales through the gaps in the window frame you should keep the curtains to retain the heat. You should also use some draught-proofing strips to minimize the nuisance.

Getting furniture for your home is usually a lifetime's work. First you buy whatever is cheap and cheerful and later you gradually up-grade. When you first move into your own place the rooms will look strangely empty and you will be glad to take any cast-offs from friends and relations that you are offered.

Much old furniture can be stripped, unless it is veneered, and either painted or stained and waxed or varnished. You can even paint wardrobes or chests of drawers and then decorate them with some freestyle painting or stencils. You may want to decorate them with wallpaper borders. Look for ideas in magazines and work out cheap ways of copying what you see in the furnishing features.

You might try what is known as découpage, which is cutting out designs from paper to make an attractive pattern, sticking it on to the furniture, then varnishing over it (many times) to protect the surface. Newspapers, pictures from magazines or brightly covered wrapping-paper can all be used in this way with great effect. Any library will have a book that tells you how to set about it. Practise on something like an old tray first until you get the hang of it.

Mirrors can add light to a room if they are placed opposite a window or hung where they reflect a light wall or an interesting view. Second-hand mirrors can be picked up fairly cheaply. You may find that the silvering has gone round the edges, but if it is not too bad the mirror will still serve you for a while (it is not usually worth having old mirrors renovated).

SAVING ENERGY

Any form of heating is expensive: the cheapest is a couple of extra woollies and a pair of thick socks, so do not automatically turn the heat up if you feel chilly. If you are sitting around watching television, wrap a blanket around your knees and put an extra jumper on before deciding whether you need to put up the temperature.

Make sure you use the heat you pay for wisely, and conserve it as much as you can. Draw curtains across the windows as it gets dark to keep the heat in. See the hot-water cylinder is well lagged – that means it has a padded jacket round it. If not, it could be worth getting one; otherwise, wrap it round with an old eiderdown or blanket. Tie the wrapping around the cylinder with strong twine. It may be worth lagging the pipes too. You can buy what you need from a good DIY store and it is very easy to do.

Draughts are uncomfortable and a waste of heat too, so invest in a roll of foam draught-proofing to seal round doors and windows. Make a 'sausage roll' to lay across the sitting-room door. Do not, in your zeal to remove draughts, block up air vents or shut out all means of air circulation. If you use gas heating or paraffin or bottled-gas heaters, or have a gas water-heater, it is vital that air can circulate. Do not use a portable paraffin or bottled-gas heater, or a gas water-heater, for long periods in a small, closed-up room. If you do, the oxygen in the room will gradually be used up and you could be overcome by carbon monoxide fumes.

Use heat only as you need it, and do not leave fires on in the bedroom, for example, when you are watching TV in another room. Do not stand furniture in front of radiators.

Hot water is probably the most expensive item of heat you will have to pay for; so if you can, take a shower instead of a bath and do not wash things under a running tap: always put a bowl in the sink first.

You can also be energy-conscious when it comes to cooking. You do not always need to pre-heat a grill, in spite of what the cookery books say, but you will find that chops take longer if you are grilling them from cold.

Do not use a small saucepan on a large gas or electric ring. You will be wasting the heat, so keep the heat under the base of the pan only. Use saucepan lids and turn the heat down as soon as you can. Do not fill kettles with more water than you need, but make sure you cover the element. Try cooking more than one vegetable in a pan. Potatoes that are nearly cooked can have green vegetables added for the last few minutes of cooking time.

If you are using the oven, try not to use it just for one thing. Cook the whole meal in it instead of just one dish, or cook an extra casserole that need only be heated through later.

So that you can check just how much electricity you are using, the reference section has full instructions on reading the meter.

KEEPING IT CLEAN

Whether you share a flat or have one to yourself, sooner or later the question of housework will rear its ugly head. Some people can remain oblivious to dust and dirt, which is infuriating if they happen to live with someone who cannot.

Most of us appreciate a clean, tidy home but do not much fancy having to maintain it.

A little maintenance every day will do for most of the time, with a real spring-clean every once in a while. Clear up newspapers, empty waste-paper baskets and ashtrays every day, and if the smell of last night's curry is still strong, fling open the windows and let the fresh air in.

Clean up the kitchen at least once a day. Wash up everything in sight and put away as many things as you can. Often storage space is rather sparse in a rented kitchen, but a large box can be used to house cleaning items, another for herbs and spices, another for cans of food, and so on, so that stores remain compact and you know more or less where to look for everything.

Keep a dustpan and brush handy to clear up messes quickly; if you spill coffee or wine on the carpet it can be removed if you set to it at once. Soda water is your best investment here, so keep some in the drinks cupboard so that you can reach for it quickly when disaster strikes.

Wine stains on carpets can generally be cleared up by flushing the stain with soda water. Blot with kitchen paper, then rub over with carpet shampoo. Wipe off with a cloth wrung out in clear water. Blot well and repeat if you need to until the stain is clear.

For coffee, mop up any residue as soon as possible, then flush out the stain with a squirt of soda water. Blot well, then sponge with warm water and blot dry.

To cope with vomit, first remove any residue with the bowl of a spoon, then rinse with soda water. Rinse with warm water and blot dry. If necessary, finish with carpet shampoo, following the manufacturer's instructions.

If you share a flat, come to an amicable arrangement with your flat-mates as to who does what. Maybe one likes housework but hates cooking. Perhaps someone else goes close to the shops on the way home from work and can shop for you all. It is best to sort out some kind of flexible rota right from the beginning. Take it in turns to clean the stairs between you and the other flats: this can be an endless source of annoyance between tenants if the chore is not shared.

Clean rubbish out regularly, for not only does refuse smell but it will encourage flies and possibly mice.

WASHING CLOTHES

Most people without a washing-machine use the launderette for the main bulk of their washing or take it home to Mum. If you have a washing-machine in your flat or hostel, spend a few minutes with the instruction book before you start using the machine. If there is no book, follow the directions on the washing-machine itself, if there are any. If in doubt wash your clothes at the very lowest temperature you can. Most clothes you buy will have a 'care' label in them and it is best to follow the advice they carry.

The chart below, from the Home Laundering Consultative Council, explains what all the symbols mean. In practical terms you will put some fabrics together with different ones to wash them, but when you do this it is prudent to wash at the lower temperature shown on the symbol.

If you are in any doubt about colourfastness, either wash the item separately by hand a few times, or wash all dark colours together until you are sure there is no leakage of colour.

Examples of application

	MACHINE	HAND WASH	
1 / **95**	Very hot to boil / maximum wash	Hand-hot or boil	White cotton and linen articles without special finishes
	Spin or wring		

	MACHINE	HAND WASH	
2 / **60**	Hot / maximum wash	Hand-hot	Cotton, linen or viscose articles without special finishes where colours are fast at 60°C
	Spin or wring		

	MACHINE	HAND WASH	
3 / **60**	Hot / medium wash	Hand-hot	White nylon; white polyester/cotton mixtures
	Cold rinse. Short spin or drip-dry		

	MACHINE	HAND WASH	
4 / **50**	Hand-hot / medium wash	Hand-hot	Coloured nylon; polyester; cotton and viscose articles with special finishes; acrylic/cotton mixtures; coloured polyester/cotton mixtures
	Cold rinse. Short spin or drip dry		

	MACHINE	HAND WASH	
5 / **40**	Warm / maximum wash	Warm	Cotton, linen or viscose articles where colours are fast at 40°C, but not at 60°C
	Spin or wring		

	MACHINE	HAND WASH	
6 / **40**	Warm / minimum wash	Warm	Acrylics; acetate and triacetate, including mixtures with wool; polyester/wool blends
	Cold rinse. Short spin. Do not wring		

	MACHINE	HAND WASH	
7 / **40**	Warm / minimum wash	Warm / Do not rub	Wool, including blankets and wool mixtures with cotton or viscose; silk
	Spin. Do not hand wring		

	MACHINE	HAND WASH	
8 / **30**	Cool / minimum wash	Cool	Silk and printed acetate fabrics with colours not fast at 40°C
	Cold rinse. Short spin. Do not wring		

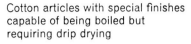

Cotton articles with special finishes capable of being boiled but requiring drip drying

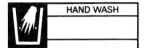

Articles which must not be machine washed. Details will vary because garment manufacturers are free to put their own written instructions on this label

Do not wash

Pressing clothes takes time but it certainly makes them look crisper and smarter. The chart shown below indicates what the various ironing symbols mean.

If in doubt, iron at a cool temperature and increase the heat slowly until you find you are getting a good result. If clothes get too dry and are difficult to iron it helps to spray them with cold water (use an indoor plant spray).

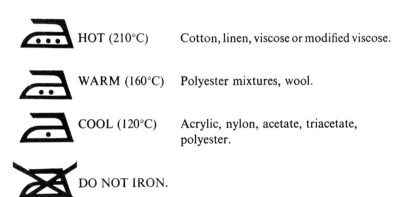

HOT (210°C)   Cotton, linen, viscose or modified viscose.

WARM (160°C)   Polyester mixtures, wool.

COOL (120°C)   Acrylic, nylon, acetate, triacetate, polyester.

DO NOT IRON.

A circle like the one shown overleaf indicates that an item can be dry-cleaned. It may contain the letters A, P or F, which indicate which solvent should be used. If the circle is underlined it means that special treatment is needed and you should point this out when you take the garment for cleaning. A cross over the circle (shown overleaf) indicates that the garment cannot be dry cleaned.

Normal goods dry-cleanable in all solvents.

 Normal goods dry-cleanable in perchloroethylene, white spirit, Solvent 113 and Solvent 11.

 Goods sensitive to dry-cleaning which may be cleaned with the same solvents shown for (P) but with a strict limitation on the addition of water during cleaning and/or certain restrictions concerning mechanical action or drying temperature or both.

 Normal goods dry-cleanable in white spirit and Solvent 113.

 Goods sensitive to dry-cleaning which may be cleaned with the same solvents shown for (F) but with a strict limitation on the addition of water during cleaning and/or certain restrictions concerning mechanical action or drying temperature or both.

 Do not dry-clean.

SAFETY IN THE HOME

Many serious accidents occur at home, nearly always to people who felt it could never happen to them.

Do not overload electrical sockets. Keep trailing flexes to a minimum (try to avoid them altogether), particularly where someone might trip.

Worn or damaged flexes should be renewed immediately. If you need an extension lead, buy a proper one, which will be both safer and much more versatile than trying to join lengths of flex.

If you climb up to reach something, take particular care to avoid standing on unstable chairs which can make you over-balance. Do not attempt to do electrical repairs unless you are qualified to do so.

If you suspect a gas leak, open the windows, turn off at the mains and call in British Gas. Their emergency number will be in the phone book, but you are advised to have a list of emergency numbers permanently pinned up near your telephone.

Fire in the home is devastating. It can start quite suddenly and spread quickly, so keep portable heaters away from furniture and curtains and position them so that they cannot be knocked over. See that oil heaters are not placed in a draught. Do not air clothes near or over a fire, or over the cooker in the kitchen.

Take care with matches and lighted cigarettes. Never smoke in bed, and see that cigarettes are never left to smoulder on the sides of armchairs or on any upholstered furniture. If you smoke, keep plenty of ash-trays around.

For fat fires, such as a blaze in an over-heated chip pan, turn off the heat, put a lid on the pan or cover the flames with a thick damp cloth or tin tray. *Do not* throw water on the pan or try to carry it outside.

If an oil stove catches fire, smother it with a large damp towel or mat. Close the door, and if you are in any doubt that you can deal with it call the Fire Brigade.

If you discover a fire, alert everyone in the building, call the Fire Brigade by dialling 999, and try to ensure everyone reaches a place of safety. Reduce draughts as far as you can. Shut all doors and windows, even in rooms away from the fire.

CHAPTER 4

A job with a future

Finding a job has never been easy and is now very much more difficult than it used to be. More and more people are chasing fewer jobs, and even for the ones that used to be easy to come by, like waitressing or working in bars, there are more applicants than vacancies.

This does not mean to say you will never find work, but it does take a good deal more effort now. This is particularly true if you have no qualifications or are lacking in confidence about what you have to offer.

Older people, for whom it was easy to get some kind of a job, can be unsympathetic simply because they do not understand the changes that have taken place over the last few years and how it is nowadays.

One of the most important things is to accept that there may be periods in your life when you will not be working. It is important to learn how to become a complete person who can enjoy leisure as well as work, not worry too much and be able to enjoy doing things whether they produce much money or not.

Before you sit down and analyse how you are going to get a job, ask yourself whether you would really like the chance to obtain more qualifications, perhaps by going to college or university, by joining a Youth Training Scheme or, if you are 19 or over, taking a TOPS course (see Chapter 11).

CHOOSING A CAREER

Some people are lucky enough to know what they want to do from an early age. With that in mind they can pick the right subjects to study and proceed in more or less a straight upward line to their goal.

Most people have a much more hazy idea of what they want to do. In some cases they are pressurized by parents into going to university or to take up a profession their parents wish they could have taken up for themselves.

Do not be haphazard about deciding what to do with the rest of your life. You need to research the possibilities thoroughly, then plan your campaign for finding a job. If you can acquire, in the course of time, an occupation which you enjoy, and which provides you with the means to live in reasonable comfort, you will have achieved a good deal.

One way out of the predicament is to go to a vocational guidance centre. However, this is not cheap: it costs about £100 for a full consultation, and consists of a series of tests, lasting about half a day, which are designed to reveal your personal potential, aptitudes and interests. Your personality is explored to discover whether you possess qualities such as leadership, independence and competitiveness, and your ability to reason or develop logical thought assessed; also analysed are the subjects in which you were strongest at school.

A personal consultation follows, at which the implications of the tests and questionnaires are explained and careers discussed. The interview may take up to two hours and if you wish them to your parents may attend.

A written report, recording the results of the tests and their implications, a summary of the interview and the recommendations of the careers advisers, is then provided.

Careers advisers are not employment agencies and cannot find you a job, but they may be used as referees.

If you cannot afford or do not like the idea of such intensive assessment, talk to as many people as possible about their jobs so that you can acquire some idea of what you might enjoy doing.

The National Advisory Centre on Careers for Women offers advice on careers and training (write to the centre for a publications list and further details).

Do not be pressurized by anyone into doing a job that you do not fancy just because the pay is good or it seems secure or your parents think it would be a good idea.

On the other hand, if you see your parents involved in jobs they love which also appear to have good prospects, stop and have a closer look at why they enjoy what they do so much and work out whether you might like to do the same.

This advice also applies to the jobs of friends. If they have found work they like, would it suit you? Or do your friends have totally different qualifications and personalities that make their jobs good for them but unsuitable for you?

Take out books on careers from the library. Haunt your careers office and look at as many leaflets on different careers as you can find. The ideal job for you could be one that you have never heard of, so you need to explore the very widest range of ideas that you can.

Look at the classified advertisement pages in newspapers to

see the range of jobs they advertise. It is worth having a look in the personal columns of some newspapers to see if any off-beat ideas for work are suggested that appeal to you.

Knowing about other people's experiences can often concentrate the mind.

Gabbie was interested in practical things and enjoyed learning to mend her motorbike, and eventually her car, more than sewing or cooking. She took three A-levels but passed only one, biology, and knew she could not go on studying.

Gabbie also knew she could never work in an office or stick to a routine job. Because of her science background (she had studied A-level maths and physics) she applied to become a trainee radio technician with the Metropolitan Police. In this job she joined the operations (technical) support group that supplies communications back-up for the police at special events, ranging from royal weddings and football matches to demonstrations and state visits.

She was able to go to college one day a week to qualify for the TEC certificate in telecommunications. Now she has that she is studying for the Higher Certificate.

Her job takes her out and about all over London and she works long, irregular hours, earning good overtime most weeks. She has learned to conquer her fear of heights as she clambers over rooftops and is resigned to being cold and wet much of the time. Now, four years later, at 23, she has become a fully-fledged radio technician and still enjoys the job – which, she says, is never the same two days running.

Joanna's Saturday job while she was at college was working in a department store. She liked the work and when she finished her course the store where she was working recommended her to write to other department stores that had a trainee scheme.

She was taken on as a management trainee in an old-established store where, to begin with, she moved around rapidly and worked in seven different departments. At the same time she went to day-release classes to study for an HNC in retail and business management.

Following the initial training she became buyer of haberdashery and knitting yarns for a year, then added dress fabrics and paper patterns to her range.

Now, five years after joining the company, she is buyer/manager of all four.

Joanna loves her work, especially the actual buying, visiting trade shows and bringing back the merchandise to watch it sell. She likes all aspects of the job but admits that paperwork is probably her least favourite.

Joanna feels there is a bright future in retailing for young people who are enthusiastic, hard-working and keen to get on. As she puts it, 'You don't have to wait until you are old to achieve results.'

Josie, on the other hand, trained as a teacher and taught in a tough comprehensive school for several years before she decided that teaching was not for her. Jobs were scarce so she took a secretarial course and got a job as a secretary, hoping it would lead to journalistic work. But in spite of working on a magazine, she found it impossible to break into journalism. The job was also poorly paid, so she moved on to other firms but never succeeded in getting out of the secretarial mould.

Fiona followed the same path, in and out of teaching. At 25 she is a temporary secretary, always hoping that the next job will give her the break she needs. Although still uncertain about her future, she is hoping for a career in public relations. She now feels that she has made a basic error in learning to type because the 'secretary' label is so difficult to leave behind.

While Josie has returned to teaching in a smaller school outside London and is now happier with the way her career is going, Fiona feels she has missed out and is uncertain what to do next.

If you do slot yourself into a job you find you do not much care for, make a resolution not to stay in it for too long, but stick at it until you can find something better and more interesting. You could consider taking time to re-train for something else. If you do not know which direction to go in, maybe vocational guidance could provide the answer. Bear in mind that changing your line of work could mean a considerable step backwards in your career aspirations: you might have to start right from the bottom again.

In the meantime the reference section provides some information about some of today's most popular careers.

ASSESSING YOUR POTENTIAL

If you have been clever at school and collected some A- and O-levels, or a clutch of CSEs, you will have a pretty fair idea about the subjects you are good at. You are probably good at them because you like them anyway, which will be a help in deciding which jobs to go after. If you have no such qualifications it does not mean you cannot do anything; it probably means that you are not academic. Everyone is good at something, so it is up to you to find out what it is in your case.

A good start is to sit down with a large sheet of paper and write down the things you like doing. You will find when you think about it that there is more to put on the list than watching TV or going swimming. You may like to mend your motorcycle, make cakes or mow the lawn for your mother. You may enjoy sewing or putting up shelves. Do not fall into the trap of thinking only about the sorts of things that used to be labelled girls' or boys' jobs. If Sharon enjoys tinkering with engines and Brian can make cakes, so much the better, because it means that there will be more job opportunities for both Sharon and Brian if they can think more broadly about the sort of jobs they want to do. Sexual discrimination in jobs is unlawful, so in theory there is nothing to prevent you taking up untraditional roles if you choose: the stumbling block is most likely to be in your own mind.

Having written down the sort of things you like doing, and any particular hobbies, think back and see whether you have had any sort of job experience in the holidays or at weekends. Perhaps you helped organize a disco at the youth club, went babysitting, worked in a shop or decorated your grandmother's sitting-room. Write it all down, because it will add up to telling a prospective employer what sort of person you are.

Once you have got a list of activities together, talk it over with your mother or father or a careers officer, or someone else whom you feel you can trust and who understands you. They may help you to think of other things to add to the list and tactfully weed out any ideas that may produce a negative reaction from a prospective employer.

Once the list is to your liking, take another sheet of paper and write on it, in your best handwriting, your name, address and date of birth, then, underneath, the schools you have attended and any examinations you have passed. If you have had work experience, in holiday jobs or otherwise, write down what you did, and for whom, then finally add your hobbies under the heading 'Interests'.

It is a good idea at this stage to put down the names of one or two people who could provide you with a reference. A prospective employer will probably ask you for one, which can be confusing if you have never had a job. He will want to hear from someone mature who can confirm that you have a good character and have not been in any kind of trouble. Employers do not normally contact referees unless they intend to give you the job. Just put down the name and address of someone you think might speak well of you. Do not forget to ask his or her permission first. The sort of person who could give you a reference might be your family doctor, your teacher or perhaps a business friend of your parents. It will not help much for your own parents to write a reference as anyone will imagine, quite justifiably, that they are prejudiced in your favour.

Once you have written this list and got it to your liking, it is worth taking a few copies of it. There is usually a photocopier at the local library or you may have a quick-print shop locally where you can get it done for quite a small charge. Keep the copies carefully, so that when you send off a job application you can enclose this sheet, universally known as a *curriculum vitae* (literally, course of life).

JOB-HUNTING

The more people who know you are looking for work, the better chance you will have of finding a job. One thing is certain: no one is going to ring you up with some fantastic offer of employment, or stop you in the street to ask if you want a job. It is up to you to go out and look for one.

If you have just left school go and see your careers officer. You will probably have been to see him earlier so the contact should be both friendly and useful. Writing down the sorts of work you would like to do, or a list of your hobbies, might help the careers officer to put you in touch with a suitable vacancy.

Haunt your local Jobcentre. Job vacancies are displayed on the boards there and they change frequently, so keep looking. If you see a job that interests you, ask the receptionist to make an appointment for you to go along for an interview.

Many job ads appear in local papers each week. They are usually listed under headings such as 'Catering', 'Secretarial', and so on, so you can find out quite quickly whether there is anything that interests you. You can find the papers in the local library so you do not need to buy any.

Look on newsagents' boards, as local firms often advertise there. You might also see a job there for something you had not thought of doing. Ask around, not just your friends or the people who live next door, but in offices or a factory where you think you might like to work. Call in and ask the receptionist whether there are any vacancies and leave a postcard with your name and address, and telephone number if you have one, so that the company can contact you. It is a good idea to add the sort of job you are looking for and any qualifications you have.

Employment agencies are a good source of office jobs, so if you can type or have other secretarial or book-keeping qualifications you may find a job there. Fees are paid by employers so the agency will not ask you for money.

In London, Capital Radio operates a scheme called Capital Jobmate. It is a Youth Unemployment Project financed by many businesses as well as the GLC, ILEA and Capital Radio itself. Anyone writing or phoning in will receive a Jobmate Kit, which is very down-to-earth and attractively presented. It takes newcomers to the job market through the whole process, from sorting out what they really want to do through to the interview and landing a job. If you live in the London boroughs covered by the scheme, you can have your own 'Job mate', who will make a personal contact with you and help you to develop the confidence and ability to land a job.

Capital Jobmate also accepts that it may be a considerable time before you land a job, and part of its goal is help and encourage unemployed people to make best use of their time. Capital Radio also operates a Jobfinder service for young people.

ANSWERING ADVERTISEMENTS

Before you answer any advertisement, read it very carefully, several times, to understand what it says about the job, and what clues it gives to the type of person the employer wants.

Do not worry if your experience does not match up exactly, though obviously if you are applying for something that needs specific qualifications or training it is not enough just to think you might be quite good at it.

If you are answering an advertisement by letter, it pays to write it out on a rough piece of paper first, to see you have included everything the ad asks for and that you have spelt everything correctly. Do not forget to put your address and telephone number and write as clearly as you can. If you are writing directly to a named person you will end the letter 'Yours sincerely', but if it is to a firm or someone identified only by job title, such as Personnel Officer, where you do not know the name, address the letter 'Dear Sir' and end it 'Yours faithfully'.

Answer any implied questions in the job advertisement in a clear, concise manner. One essential is to see that everything is spelt correctly, including the name of the firm. Even the most benevolent employer is put off by seeing words mis-spelt and it could be that he will consign your letter to the wastepaper bin.

For many jobs advertised there is just a phone number to ring.

Before you put through a call make sure you know who you want to speak to, or if the advertisement did not give a name, the job you are enquiring about. If you are in a phone-box make sure you have enough money to cover the call. Have a pen and paper handy to write down any instructions you may be given. Be ready to put yourself across well, sound cheerful and confident, and speak clearly.

When you get through, write down any details about the job so that you can think about them before you go to an interview. Make sure you have written down the day and time you are to go, and the name of the person to contact. Check you have the full address. If you do not know where it is, ask how to get there.

Be pleasant and try to sound friendly on the phone. If you have a bad line and cannot hear properly, it is better to say you will ring back rather than get annoyed or flustered. When you have all the information, repeat the time and place of the interview, then say goodbye and put down the phone.

If you have written a letter of application, do not expect a quick answer. Unfortunately a large number of firms do not reply at all. This may be for a variety of reasons: it could be laziness, but is more likely overwork or the sheer volume of replies received. I once had 450 replies to a vacancy for a trainee journalist, and it would have been very costly and time-consuming to answer them all. I felt badly about all the disappointment caused but the work one does for any company or organization must justify the cost involved in carrying it out. The important thing is not to get too despondent if you do not hear anything. Try not to take it personally and keep on writing: grow a second skin.

Many employers will telephone if they are interested in your application, so try to cultivate a bright, enthusiastic telephone voice and use it every time you answer the phone. If you are sharing the phone with others, especially if a younger brother or sister might answer, do impress on everyone that you may get an important phone call, and that if it comes through they should write the message down and leave it somewhere where you will find it easily.

THE INTERVIEW

When you finally get an interview, do not panic, but do not think the job is all but yours. Most employers will interview a dozen people or more and you may be interviewed by someone in the personnel department first, whose job will be to weed out the more unsuitable applicants so the boss is left with just a shortlist.

If you are given an appointment, make sure you know who you should ask for when you arrive and, if it is a large firm, the department in which he or she works. Find out how to get to the building, and if it is some distance away work out how long it will take to get there; also check you have enough money on you to get there and back.

Leave yourself plenty of time. The ideal time to arrive for an appointment is about five minutes early. Five minutes late is not good enough. It will create a bad impression even though you may be kept waiting for fifteen minutes in the reception area.

It is not old-fashioned to say it is important to dress for the occasion. If you are going to do heavy outdoor work, jeans may be appropriate, but, even so, it is better if they are clean jeans with a tidy, newish sweater. The whole idea is to look as if you would value the job if you got it, and that you have made some kind of effort for the occasion.

If you are going for an office job, it is more important to dress suitably. Wear something you feel good in but not sexy – no low-cut blouses. Check that tights are ladder-free, shoes as clean as possible, handbag well cared for and clothes clean and uncrumpled. See your hair is tidy and make-up, if you use it, is suitable for the occasion. None of this advice is to suggest that you should look like something you are not, but any prospective employer who has many other people to choose from will want to feel that you care about the job enough to have made some effort.

When you are finally ushered through the door to the interview, remember that first impressions count. Take a deep breath, stand up straight, do not slouch, and look your interviewer straight in the eye. Smile. Be prepared to shake hands if a hand is profferred and do not sit down until you are invited to do so. Any experienced interviewer will do his or her best to put you at ease during the first few minutes, for until you are reasonably relaxed you will not be able to sit and chat easily, which is when a skilled person will be finding out the sort of person you are.

Do not sink into the chair and reach for a cigarette – that could lose you the job. At best, wait until invited to smoke, but even then, unless the person interviewing you is also smoking it is better to say no. I have worked for people who would not take on anyone who smokes: that may sound unfair, but if you have a job on offer you are in a position to make such conditions, and it is important to remember that one smoker affects the whole working environment.

At the beginning of an interview you will be asked easy questions ranging from 'How long did it take you to get here?' to 'How long ago did you leave school?' Do not think it strange if the answers to some of these questions are already clearly stated in your letter of application; this is merely a way of easing you into the more serious part of the interview.

Try to answer questions with more than a straight yes or no.

The interviewer will be wanting to know whether you can communicate, what your background is and how you are likely to fit in with the people already in the firm, as well as whether you could actually do the job. Do not lie about any qualification or job experience. It is not worth it, as you will almost certainly be discovered later.

You will probably be asked about matters not strictly connected with your job, like whether you are planning to get married, whether you live at home and what your hobbies are.

The most usual areas for an interviewer to cover are your background, family interests, and so on: strictly factual subjects, like the schools you attended and any qualifications you may have. The interviewer will also want to discover your own hopes and aspirations for the future. One fairly common question might be 'What would you like to be doing in five years' time?' and although you may have only the vaguest idea it is as well to be prepared for the question and give some kind of answer. Another question that might throw you off balance is 'Why do you think you could do this particular job?' Here you will have to think quickly, bearing in mind what the interviewer has told you about the job over the last twenty minutes, and apply it to what you feel are your own skills. For example, if the job involves filing, you can emphasise the fact that you helped in the school library, or that you feel you are methodical.

Try to sound enthusiastic throughout the interview and look at the person who is talking to you – this is called eye-contact. It is very important not to talk to the ground or a piece of wall behind the interviewer's head.

Take your time answering questions. Do not worry too much if there is a silence while you think out a reply. This may not be ideal, but it is better than blurting out something silly, whereas a few seconds would have given you time to think.

Be straightforward in your answers. If you try to duck out of a question or evade giving a truthful answer it will be very obvious, and to an interviewer might seem worse than it is. If you do not know the answer to a question and you cannot think of anything, it is best to admit it.

An important aspect of the interview which people new to the game often overlook is that an interview is a two-way affair. It is a big step for you to get a job and to enter an environment where you will spend anything up to 40 hours a week, probably for several years to come. You want to know that you will enjoy it, that the job has some prospects for promotion and that the conditions of employment are fair and reasonable.

Look around the offices. Are they clean and fresh or dirty and murky? Are the other people you met on the way in of your own age or much older? Do they look fairly happy? Is the office furniture in reasonable condition or are you sitting on a wobbly chair? Does the person interviewing you look as if he or she would care about you beyond how much work they could get out of you?

Conditions of work are about more than holidays and what time you start in the morning. They concern the quality of your working life as well. You may not be able to pick work you enjoy wholeheartedly at the beginning when you are striking out, so it is more important than ever to like the other aspects of the job – the people you work with and the overall atmosphere of the place.

Most employers are impressed if you ask questions about the firm itself, or the prospects of promotion once you are in the job. Some firms have recognized training schemes, sometimes day-release programmes. Others will expect you to take evening classes for additional qualifications. Find out what opportunities there are for you to get on. (Read more about making progress in your career in Chapter 5.)

When the interview is over, the interviewer is most likely to say, 'Thank you for coming, we'll let you know.' If no indication is given as to how soon it will be, you could ask. Otherwise, just smile, shake hands if a hand is profferred and leave the room. Do not forget to shut the door!

You may have to wait some time before the results of your interview are known. Unfortunately, in some cases you will not hear anything. But do not be too dismayed. You will have to get used to the techniques of job interviewing (and remember when it comes to your turn to interview potential staff the way you would like to have been treated yourself).

GETTING THE JOB

One magic day you will receive an offer of employment and accept it. Then you will fix a day to start, and finally you will arrive in your new workplace.

It will take time for you to settle in and stop feeling strange. You will almost certainly feel extremely tired when you first begin work. For a start you will have a longer working day, and in contrast to school or college, where you frequently stop one activity and start another, you may find yourself sitting at a desk for most of the day without any real excuse to get up and move around.

Most people have to travel to their work, and fighting your way on to public transport during rush hours will be tiring too.

It may take you some time to learn your way around your place of work – you may even get lost in a maze of corridors – and you will not know who everyone is at first. But gradually it will all make sense and after the first month or so you will feel like an old hand.

Get yourself into the attitude of mind where you play fair with your employer. It is very easy to waste time during the day – your employer's time – in chatting to colleagues and making private phone calls, but this can cause considerable annoyance. Most employers do not object to private calls being made if there is a special need, but do not abuse the privilege by organizing your social life on the company's time. Similarly, it is only fair to keep to the regular hours and the lunch time allowed and not keep arriving late, in the mornings or after lunch. Anyone who consistently arrives late pushes extra work and responsibility on to all the others who arrive on time, and is simply not playing fair with his or her employer.

Although you have to attend the office day after day for the required number of hours you may not always be busy. In some jobs there are times when there is little to do, and this can become extremely boring. If this does occur, try to use the time profitably to find out more about your industry or field of work. Look around and see what else needs to be done – perhaps for someone else who is extremely busy. On other days you will be rushed off your feet and wonder how you can cope, but these fluctuations in work patterns occur in all jobs, even for those at the top, and after a while you will get used to the irregular work-flow and think nothing of it.

Find out all you can about what is going on around you, beyond your own job, within your own department or area and in the larger context of the organization. It will help you to assess whether you are happy to stay in the department where you started or whether you would like to make a move within the firm, should a vacancy occur.

Make the most of any facilities on offer. If there is a canteen use it; it provides a chance to meet and chat to the people you work with in a relaxed way. There may be social facilities. Some firms run keep-fit classes during the lunch hour, or have a social club. You may wish to get involved in trade union activities. Watch the notice boards – a good source of information about what is going on within the company. Usually job vacancies, promotions within the company and events connected with after-hours clubs are advertised. If there is no notice board, make a name for yourself and suggest that one should be made available.

TERMS AND CONDITIONS

Once you have accepted a job, both you and your employer are bound by the terms offered and agreed. Under the employment protection legislation your employer must give you, within 13 weeks of starting work, a written statement of your terms and conditions. (Normally you will receive it within a couple of weeks.) If you are not given one within 13 weeks, ask why not.

You must keep this written statement, your contract of employment, very carefully in a safe place so that you can refer to it when necessary. If you are involved in any sort of dispute later on, you will need to refer to it and possibly produce it as evidence.

This letter or form must state:

(1) your salary, and how it is calculated, including terms for overtime pay, if any;

(2) how often the payment is to be made (e.g. monthly or weekly);

(3) terms and conditions relating to hours of work, including normal working hours;

(4) terms relating to holiday entitlement and holiday pay, pensions and pension schemes and provisions for sick pay;

(5) how much notice you must give if you want to leave or how much notice you should be given in the event of dismissal or redundancy.

If the contract is for a set period only it should state the date of expiry.

Your contract will also state the title of the job you are employed to do. In addition it should list provisions made for disciplinary and grievance procedure, or, if not, tell you where these can be found. You may find, for example, that the boss's secretary or the personnel department keeps them, but they should be easily available to anyone who wants them.

The provision of a written statement is not necessary for anyone who is not an employee: for example, those who work on a freelance basis and pay their own insurance stamps, or employees who normally work less than 16 hours a week, unless they have been employed continuously by the same organization for at least 8 hours a week for the last 5 years.

SICK PAY

Even the most healthy of us can break an ankle, or catch 'flu. If you are absent through illness, your employer is obviously not gaining any benefit from employing you and may therefore not wish to carry on paying your wages.

Some companies carry on paying their staff during a period of sickness, up to a maximum period. But many other companies cannot or do not wish to afford this, so the government has introduced Statutory Sick Pay (known as SSP); this compels employers to pay you a minimum daily wage, related to your salary, which they can then reclaim from the government.

Rules for calculation of SSP are notoriously complicated. In essence, no SSP is paid during the first three days of a spell of sickness; SSP is then payable for all subsequent working days on which you remain sick, up to a maximum of 8 weeks in one year.

It is up to you and your employer to agree what constitutes sickness. During the first week of sickness, you may be asked to write yourself a sick note, and during subsequent weeks to present a doctor's certificate.

HEALTH AND SAFETY

Your employer or supervisor should tell you about the health and safety regulations relative to your place of work. If he does not, ask. You can also obtain advice from trade union representatives, if there is a union. Find out, particularly if you work in a factory or other industrial environment, how to work safely. Always obey safety rules, and if you are issued with protective clothing, wear it. Get treatment for any injury, however slight, report it to your supervisor and see that it is recorded in the accident book.

If you take time off work because of an injury that happened at work ask the doctor for a certificate you can send to your employer. You could be entitled to Industrial Injury benefit. (Ask for leaflet NI6 from your local DHSS.)

JOINING A UNION

Once you are 16 you are entitled to join a trade union. Some industries have more union involvement than others and only you can decide whether or not to join.

If your only view of trade unions is watching television or reading the headlines in the newspapers you might think that joining one means endlessly going on strike or standing on picket lines. But the majority of trade unions are not in a constant state of confrontation or dispute. They look after their members' interests by negotiation and discussion with the employers.

If there is a trade union or unions (sometimes there are several unions operating within one workplace) where you work you will probably be approached and asked to join. If you do, you will pay a regular subscription towards union funds and will be expected to attend meetings and join in discussions on how your union is run. The union will negotiate on pay increases and will normally take up grievances on your behalf. It will also negotiate for better terms and conditions, or defend existing ones under threat, and resist redundancies.

In many instances there is an agreement that all workers will belong to a union and you will be expected to join. In rarer cases, you may find that you cannot get a job within a company or industry unless you belong to the union, but on the other hand you may not be able to join unless you have a job in the first place.

If you have strong views about not joining a union you cannot be pressurized into doing so, but you may find that your colleagues resent the fact that you get all the advantages of the union presence without having to pay its fees.

PAYMENT OF WAGES

When you first begin work, whether you are paid weekly or monthly, you will have to wait for your wages. If this causes hardship you may be able to claim supplementary benefit for the period you are waiting. Enquire at your local DHSS office.

When the great moment finally comes for you to receive your money or salary cheque it should be accompanied by a payslip itemizing the exact amount you have earned and detailing any deductions (if the money is paid directly into your bank account you will still receive a payslip, as confirmation).

This statement is required by law; the few exceptions usually relate to freelance and part-time employment (the latter normally of less than 16 hours a week, unless the employee has been employed continuously by the same organization for at least 8 hours a week for at least 5 years).

There are a few other exceptions, so if your money comes without a detailed account, ask why.

The pay statement must record the following:

(1) gross amount of wages (i.e. total amount before deductions);

(2) amount of and reason for any fixed deductions, such as trade union subcriptions, national savings scheme contributions and pension contributions;

(3) amount of and reason for any variable deductions such as income tax or National Insurance contributions;

(4) net pay (the amount you are left with after all deductions).

The payslip will probably also state the amount of tax, national insurance and superannuation (pension) contributions that you have paid in the tax year to date, and your tax code number.

If you have any queries ask your supervisor or the personnel department.

EQUAL OPPORTUNITIES

Employers are not allowed to discriminate on grounds of sex or race in their recruitment or their treatment of you as an employee, nor in promotion or training provision. It is also unlawful to discriminate against employees who are married.

If you are a woman doing work of equal value to that of a man working for the same employer, even though your job might not have been assessed under a job evaluation scheme, you are entitled to the same terms of employment, including pay, as a man.

The Sex Discrimination Act and the Equal Pay Act apply to both manual and non-manual work, full-time and part-time, whether in factories, offices, shops or anywhere else.

Knowing you should be paid the same rate for the job as a man and actually getting it are two different things. Some industries, such as journalism, have a good record on the equal pay front. But this is by no means true of all jobs. One of the problems is often that you cannot find out how much other people do earn, as in Britain people tend to be extremely secretive in these matters.

You may be able to find out by asking informally around the office from your friends. If you belong to a trade union you should be able to find out from your branch officer if you are being paid in line with men who are doing the same kind of job. Failing that, have a word with your personnel department. If you get nowhere, and have serious suspicions that you are earning less, contact the Equal Opportunities Commission, which may be able to give you advice or find out for you.

Their leaflet *Equal Pay for Women* gives more details, and they also have other helpful leaflets, all free.

NOTICE TO QUIT

If your employer gives you notice to quit you should remember you have certain rights: if you have worked for the firm for one month or more but less than two years you are entitled to one week's notice; you must be given at least two weeks' notice if you have been employed continuously for two years, and a week extra for each complete year of service up to 12 years, including any period when you have been on holiday or sick leave. The period of notice may be worked, or you may be given pay in lieu of notice. If you have been dismissed for what is generally know as gross misconduct, such as stealing, you can be asked to leave at once.

If you have been employed on a fixed-term contract, that is, a job with a time-limit (a set number of years, months or weeks), no period of notice is required at the end of the fixed term. Apprentices and trainees are normally treated as employees on fixed-term contracts, so the same rules apply.

If you are dismissed, you are entitled to be given the reason in writing, provided you have worked for your employer for at least six months, but you must ask for it. This is important, especially if you decide to complain of unfair dismissal.

LEAVING YOUR JOB
For advice on moving on to a new job, see Chapter 5 ('Moving On', pages 62–4).

On the day you leave or shortly afterwards you should be paid all outstanding wages including overtime and any extra money in lieu of holidays not taken. You will be given a P45, a tax record, to use for claiming benefit or to give to your next employer, and a P60, stating how much income tax you have paid to date in the current tax year.

UNFAIR DISMISSAL
If you feel you have been unfairly dismissed, you should seek advice from an expert – immediately; do not wait, or you may lose your rights. Some lawyers offer a free advice service for this situation.

Otherwise, your trade union, if you belong to one, or the Citizens' Advice Bureau or a Neighbourhood Advice Centre, may be able to help (find out where the latter are from your local library or the phone book).

If you have worked for your employer for 52 weeks or more without a break, other than holiday or sick leave, you may complain to an industrial tribunal if you think your dismissal was unfair. The time qualification does not apply if you think you were dismissed for belonging to a union, or for not joining one, or if you were dismissed because of your race or sex.

If you are on a Youth Training Scheme you cannot be dismissed but you may be suspended. If your work or conduct is unsatisfactory the employer may complain to the Careers Service or the Manpower Services Commission, who would most likely try to find you another placement.

CHAPTER 5

Onward and upward

Getting on in the job you have found is more than a question of performing well. There are other skills that you will need to identify and develop if you want to go up the ladder.

You will need to get on with the people you work with – not just your boss, but the people in between you and your boss, as well as your colleagues, the tea-lady, the post-room boy and the customers you might meet as part of your job.

You must learn how to play the company game, perform well at meetings, survive office politics and understand business etiquette.

Most big firms have organization charts, a sort of family tree of the company's staffing structure. Sometimes in a big company, the personnel department will give you one on your first day at work, and occasionally you will have a chart drawn in on your job description. In smaller firms, especially where there is only a handful of staff, you will have to work it out for yourself.

But the official organization chart is one thing; the unofficial chart, the one that shows you who has the real power, is often quite different.

Power may be in quite different hands. It may be that the boss's personal assistant has an influence on who gets pointed out for promotion and the secretary will certainly have a say in who gets easy access to the chief. Someone in a comparatively lowly position may be related to the chairman, or the harrassed person in the accounts department may be the one who signs and passes all the expenses. Anyone who can effectively block or hold up expenditure is important.

Look at who meets whom outside the office. Some people will play squash together, some will go to the theatre or have mutual friends that mean they meet outside normal working hours. They may belong to the same club. Informal meetings outside the office forge important links for the future.

Some workplaces are more political than others, but in all organizations with more than a few employees quite a lot of manoeuvring goes on behind the scenes, and in some *whom* you know is certainly more important than *what* you know. Do not imagine that just being good at the job is all you need to achieve instant recognition.

WORKMATES

Getting on with your colleagues at work is just as important as getting on with your boss. Liking people and being liked in return is not only an important life skill but essential if you are to make progress in your career.

Being well thought of does not mean always going along with the crowd. It is possible to succeed without alienating those around you. Being straightforward and not resorting to devious tricks makes people learn to trust you and eventually to accept that you may be moving on ahead and leaving them behind. It is important to show that you are not planning to tread all over everyone in your way to the top. Giving a colleague a hand with something they find difficult is a kindness – and disarming, too, as long as you do not harp on it for ever afterwards.

If you are going to run ahead of the rest you must accept that some jealousy is inevitable. Learn to recognize this and not let it rile you. Do not accept praise and seemingly helpful advice without analysing whether or not it is genuine. There will always be someone who wants to see you fall flat on your face, so learn to live with it and do not let it needle you into performing less well.

If you believe in yourself sufficiently you will be able to ignore the pinpricks. Try not to show colleagues in an unfavourable light, and if anyone lets you down do not go running to your superior to tell tales. You may find, if you are not careful, that by showing you are willing to accept extra responsibility you may be off-loaded with other people's work. It is a tricky situation to handle. On the one hand, you do not want to refuse to help a colleague out of a jam; on the other hand, their passing extra work on to you could easily become a habit.

If you really feel that you are being used, the best thing is to bring it out into the open and say you are sorry but you cannot take on that extra work because you are fully occupied with your own.

DO YOU HAVE A 'GOOD' BOSS?

Your relationship with your immediate superior is a subtle one and whatever you think of him you should, at least on the surface, keep a regular rapport between you.

A boss, above all, hopes for and expects loyalty from subordinates. If you have clashes, see that they are conducted in private, not at meetings or anywhere else where one of you can lose face.

Always remember that the boss is a human being too. He has pressures outside the office as well as those within. He wants to do well in his own job and if he can see that you can assist him on his route to the top your own prestige will be enhanced.

He will respond to a person who is efficient and helps him do his own job better: someone who can follow through a project, obtain facts and present them simply, at whatever level. A friendly, cheerful face around the office is always welcome, as is someone who can keep cool and contribute positively when there is a crisis. Does all this sound like you?

Do not sabotage your boss's work behind his back. Being loyal means not being drawn into criticism of the work your chief is doing, either by your own colleagues or by other department heads who may throw out the odd random remark just to see how you react.

It will not take you long to discover that no boss is perfect. Some are terrible managers, and they may be only reasonably efficient themselves. The reasons for this are varied, but the most likely explanation is that their own bosses before them were pretty indifferent as well, and they were not trained in management skills.

One important point to note is how well a job is explained to you when it is allocated. Unless you are given all the facts at the time it may be difficult or even impossible to complete the task effectively. You may be given an unrealistic timescale for the project. Help your boss by asking if you do not understand what you are expected to do, or if you do not have all the background information you need. People will very rarely give you misleading or inadequate information purposely, but it may be that they have not thought the job through in their own minds, or have never performed the task themselves and do not know what is involved.

If you are asked to finish the work by an impossible deadline, say so at the start, rather than risk running late and being unable to deliver.

Beware the boss who wants to be everybody's friend. It means he feels insecure in that he has to be liked by one and all. When you become a boss yourself you will discover that it just is not possible. No one can go out with the people working under them for a gossip and a drink at lunchtime, then take the same group to task for sloppy work in the afternoon.

The most important feeling you should have for the person you work for is respect: respect for his knowledge and judgement. Take note of his relationship with his own superiors as well as colleagues at his own level. Here again the word 'respect' is all important. Do they appear to be going places, or is your boss himself last in the promotional line? If so, do not spend too long in that particular job as it could and probably will turn out to be a dead end.

Is your boss loyal to people who work for him as well as to the company? If not, you may find that, unknown to you, your own prospects are being sabotaged behind your back.

A concerned boss will be keen to see you get on and will take time to have regular chats with you about your performance. In some companies there is a formal appraisal scheme, for which you will be asked to fill in a form or take tests to assess your work performance.

What might happen is that your personnel department will send you a form listing various questions about your job, such as 'What part of your job have you found most difficult?', 'What part of your work do you like best?' or 'What do you think you have achieved in the last year?' Your immediate chief will also have a form on which to write an assessment of your work performance as well as a summary of your potential for the future, and will be able to suggest any particular training from which you could benefit. You will then have a chance to sit down with them, read the review and discuss it. Some appraisal forms require you to sign to say you have read the comments; you will also be given the opportunity to add comments of your own if you feel you have been misrepresented.

On the whole, this more formal appraisal system applies to large companies or government departments, but in most offices there is a chance to sit down with your employer from time to time to discuss your work and how you are 'getting on'. If not, create your own opportunity. Ask if you can make an appointment to discuss how you are doing. Make a list of any points you want to raise, such as the opportunity for extra training either on the job or on an outside course.

Be prepared for a few home truths. Criticism is always uncomfortable, but even if you feel at the time it is unfair or unjustified, try to put a good face on it, then go away to think about it. It is a fact of life that if you are performing well in your job you will rarely get a word of praise, but if you slip up you will very soon get to know about it. So do not become the sort of person who expects a shower of compliments every time a task is finished.

SETTING GOALS

Setting realistic goals is important in planning your career. It is vital to stretch yourself and aim high, but not so high that the task is impossible and you are doomed to fail.

Many people just drift into a job and never bother to drift out again. They quite like the work, they quite like the conditions and they quite like the people. But for those who are ambitious drifting is not enough.

Sit down one day and write down what you hope to be doing in five years' time. You may know immediately but you may find that you pause to think more carefully.

What do you expect to be earning in five years? What sort of lifestyle do you hope to achieve? Will you have a partner or do you expect to be still solo? Do you want to work all your life in the same geographical area or have you ever thought you might like to work abroad or in another part of the country?

Anyone embarking on a career in the uncertain 1980s is likely to have at least one if not more changes of career during his or her working life.

You may find that by writing down what you want to be doing in five or ten years that you are questioning your job and many possible promotions. You may even query whether you are in the right kind of work at all.

How much does money mean to you? Money in itself means little to most people; it is what it can do that counts.

We are most often judged by what we acquire through money: the size of our house, the clothes we buy, the car we drive or the type of holidays we take. What is emerging now however, amongst more and more people, is a much healthier attitude: that wealth matters much less than the quality of life it enables you to achieve.

For some the quality they need may still be the excitement of the big city, the cut-and-thrust of getting ahead in the job and winning all the races they can run. Others may prefer to take things, including their ambitions and their career, more slowly. If you know that you are in the latter group you will never be happy struggling in the ranks of the go-getters for whom the top job in the company is the only worthwhile goal.

Acknowledge the fact and be prepared to accept that you will play a supportive rather than the chief executive role in your career. It does not make you any less of a success as a person; it means that you have set different sights for yourself.

TAKING A SUPPORTING ROLE

If you do find yourself in a supporting rather than a dominating role, it is more important than ever to be working for a person with the flair and dynamism to get to the top and take you with him. You may be working alongside a budding, or fully-fledged, entrepreneur.

The true entrepreneurs of this world are usually highly individualistic. They know where they are going and may blatantly use people to achieve their ends. They can be difficult, arrogant, fickle and totally disarming. They have the flair and vision to make their dream a reality but they need a back-up team or individual to do the essential background work and to attend to mundane details. Do you know or work for someone in that mould? Entrepreneurs are usually best working for themselves, but very often they cut their teeth and gain experience in a large organization where they probably make a lot of enemies. They are different. They can rock the boat, they rough-ride over people and may make even the chairman feel uncomfortable. So if, in a large company, you are too closely associated with one you may find that when he disappears rather suddenly you are quick to follow.

Beware of identifying yourself too closely with anyone in particular. Be your own person and unless you are convinced that you can follow the mercurial executive wherever he goes, stand back a bit, or you may find yourself job-hunting sooner than you expected.

Most bosses are less spectacular, however, and perform well without being outstanding. In most companies managers are reasonably efficient and in larger companies they often acquire an Identi-Kit that you will learn to recognize. In such companies you will have more to do with your department head than the managing director, and as he moves ahead within the company you may well progress with him.

INTERNAL COMMUNICATIONS

Every company has its own way of writing memos – and that does not mean how they set out the page. In many companies memos fly around the building like demented pigeons and fill up the filing cabinets for years. Some executives spend more time writing them than in getting on with their main function. Memos certainly have their place, in confirming information received or decisions taken, but they can become sensitive if used for stating personal views on any topic.

The most important thing to remember when you start to put pen to paper is that you are placing your views on a particular situation on permanent record. So rule no. 1 is not to write anything in haste, especially after a frustrating meeting or after a brush with a colleague. It is better to leave repartee or biting wit for another time and place, as it can make for embarrassing reading on file for months, if not years, to come.

Complaints about a colleague or a contentious view of something that has happened may be sent to the person named for their comments, and can often rebound on you.

Long memos are rarely read, so keep yours short and to the point. Write concisely, and if in doubt check the spelling, particularly of people's names. Get job titles right too. No one is going to concentrate on what you have said if his name is mis-spelt and his job wrongly described.

Be factual and always polite, even when you feel annoyed. If you expect a reply to your memo, couch a question in such a way that it cannot be ignored. Give a deadline for the answer too.

The same rules apply when writing letters to people outside the company. Present your letter well and check that it is accurately typed. Check up on your own company style for business letters and stick to the formula. Be concise in what you say and use normal, everyday language. Plan what to say before you write and see that the points you make are in logical order.

PROJECTING YOURSELF AT WORK

If you have to give commands, make them to the point so that no one is in any doubt about what you mean. Do not start with an apology or phrase such as 'I know you are busy, but when you get a minute would you. . .'. The chances are that the person will never find that minute, and if he or she is feeling bolshy or over-stressed your request will be ignored. The direct approach ('This has to be done today, so could you please let me know when it's finished?') leaves no one in any doubt at all that you mean business.

Performing well at internal meetings is one of the quickest ways to get yourself noticed within a company. Many people who have seen you around will not know much about you until they see you in this situation.

When you are asked to attend a meeting always find out what will be discussed. (If an agenda has been circulated, so much the better.) Be prepared. Do some homework on the topics to be discussed so that you have a view about what is happening even if no one asks your opinion.

As children many of us were brought up to wait until other people had finished speaking before we spoke, and not to contradict. Applying such rules to the average management meeting could mean you will never open your mouth.

If you have a point to make you must be prepared to leap in when you have an opportunity and put your point of view with authority. Do not be hesitant about what you have to say and do not preface every sentence with an apology. Many people, through nervousness, present their ideas with phrases like 'I know it's probably not relevant but . . .' or 'It probably won't work, but . . .' – which positively invite a negative reaction. On the other hand, avoid an over-strident approach – that will alienate your colleagues.

If you find you never command attention at meetings or people just ignore what you say, consider *how* you say things. Do you talk with conviction? And do you pitch your voice low – but not so low that no one can hear you?

Avoid expressions such as 'you know' or clichés such as 'It's just a thought, but . . .' I worked for years with a colleague who prefaced everything he said with that phrase. We were all so conscious of it that we rarely heard the rest of the sentence.

If someone asks your opinion, state your case factually and leave any passion or emotion for another time and place. Do not be afraid to state your views whether you are asked or not. Colleagues will want to know what you think or they would not have asked you to attend, but do not interrupt others when they are making a point. If your boss is with you be prepared to make way for him to speak.

When you disagree with something, do not launch into a full-frontal attack. People feel very sensitive at meetings and no one enjoys losing face. If you think a project should be tackled differently it is better to say, 'That's one way of doing it, but have you thought of doing it this way?' It will be better received than a flat 'That will never work'. On the other hand, if someone makes such a remark to you, do not overreact. Do not get angry, and try to maintain a positive attitude. Stick to your guns and reconfirm your views and the reasons for them.

Obviously things will not always go your way and you will soon develop an instinct for when to give in or change direction without making it an obvious capitulation. Watch other, more experienced, team members at work at meetings and take your cues from them. You will learn a lot from watching and listening to them.

SOCIAL GRACES

Socializing, with either your colleagues or your customers, is another aspect of getting on in the job, and one that you should not ignore.

Although the bond you have in common is bound to be your

work, at least at the beginning, it is a dull person who can only talk about business.

As you go up into junior or middle management you may be expected to take customers out to lunch, attend charity dinners or entertain in restaurants, or even in your own home.

Right from the beginning, make sure you remember the name of people's partners, whether they have children, and any background information that they may happen to reveal to you, such as a passion for gardening, or a holiday home in Spain. One executive I know used to keep an address book listing such facts and it certainly paid off when he remembered business contacts' birthdays, and when their children had taken exams. It is not a joke when people say that a lot of profitable business is done on the golf course or after a game of squash. Cultivate the right hobbies, learn where you can acquire tickets for Wimbledon, rugby internationals or good seats for the theatre to beguile and enhance your standing with useful contacts.

No one will succeed by these methods alone, but with competition for better jobs getting more and more keen, it is these extra talents that may count in your favour.

CONVERSATIONAL SKILLS
Learn the art of conversation. Do not think that because you are with business colleagues you should talk only about work. On semi-social occasions it can be very off-putting if someone talks contracts in your ear. There is a time and a place for everything and being able to talk about other, wider issues is very important. One of the best ways to keep abreast of events is to read more than one newspaper and, ideally, read them from cover to cover including the sports and the business sections. Read cinema and theatre reviews so that even if you have not seen a film or play you can at least discuss it. Keep an open, interested mind about everything, so that when you find yourself with a bridge fanatic, someone who grows orchids or a campaigner for lead-free petrol you can ask sensible questions. If you do not know much about a subject, it is best to say so rather than try to flannel through. Someone with an absorbing hobby or strong convictions concerning animal rights will be only too keen to discuss them with you.

If you are taking someone to lunch on business you should aim to keep the best seat at the table for your guest, so that if anyone has to be jostled by the waiter or face the wall it is you. Confine the conversation to small talk at the beginning and gradually bring the subject round to the matter in question.

Sometimes you will have to socialize with people who are a lot older than you, which can be a daunting experience. Try to have in your mind some topics of conversation that you feel will be of mutual interest right from the start, so that you can feel at ease with each other as quickly as possible. Above all, be courteous and tolerant. Some older people *can* be bores, but so too can younger ones.

MOVING ON

Moving around in the early part of your career makes sense. Sooner or later you will feel that going to another company will give you the sort of promotion, or the salary boost, that is not immediately attainable in your present company – where, perhaps, you will always be labelled a beginner because that is where you started out. You may wish to gain a different sort of experience from that which you have had to date, or you may simply be unhappy or frustrated with the work you are doing, without being able to manoeuvre, or with your boss or colleagues.

Avoid resigning in a fit of pique. There may be times in your career when the urge to do so is very strong, but such a step will harm only you, not the company from which you resign – and you could find your hasty resignation difficult and embarrassing to explain away later if the word gets round.

Having decided to go, you will start looking seriously at job advertisements, making use of your contacts within your field, sending out a few exploratory letters 'on spec.' to organizations for which you would like to work given the right circumstances.

Try not to quit your present job before you have a new position confirmed: it is much easier to negotiate a new employment deal from the position of being in work, and therefore not desperate, than from being unemployed.

A sensitive supervisor might get 'vibes' from you that you are restless before you announce that you have found another job. Your office friends may have leaked the secret (far better not to tell them at all until you have been offered, and have accepted, a new job), and if you start to wear what may jokingly become known as your 'interview outfit' and disappear at odd times people will soon realize that you hope to be on the move.

Within reason, this will be tolerated as long as you continue to do your job efficiently: remember, your 'old' company is still paying you for a job of work.

When you are job-hunting most prospective employers will appreciate the need for discretion and not ask for references until the new position has been offered and accepted, subject to satisfactory references.

If you answer advertisements for which the contact is a box number, you should ask the addressee not to send your application to your present company (nor to any others to which you would not wish to apply).

Once the new job is confirmed (that is, you have agreed terms and received confirmation of the job offer in writing), you will need to give in your notice. Normally an informal note is best, along the lines of:

Dear . . . ,

I write to give you . . . weeks' notice of my resignation from my job as junior technician. Although I have been very happy here I feel it is time to move on and gain more experience.

Yours sincerely,

This is the sort of note that most supervisors would appreciate receiving. See your boss and give him the note: 'This is my resignation, I'm afraid,' is all you need say by way of explanation. In normal circumstances you will have a chance to discuss the matter and explain why you want to leave, and perhaps you might take this opportunity to try to negotiate an earlier leaving date, if you want one. Aim to keep the relationship friendly. In many industries you could end up working for or with the same person again at a later stage in your career.

Informal chats at this stage should not be construed as opportunities to deliver home truths, however much you might be tempted to do so. It just is not worth it, especially as you may have to negotiate pay in lieu of holidays not taken, outstanding bonus or overtime payments, etc.

It is not absolutely essential to write a letter of resignation; you can inform your supervisor verbally, although putting it on paper is more efficient and prevents misunderstandings. Take your cue from how other people in the company have resigned. If you feel you have only just given in your notice before you would have been fired, or you have been in open conflict with the company, it might be best to write a letter and leave it at that, or explain the situation to your personnel department.

The period of notice you are required to give will be stated in your contract of employment (see page 48) but will be a minimum of one week, which you can give on any day of the week to expire one week later unless your contract states otherwise. If you gave notice on a Monday afternoon it would be effective as from the following day, Tuesday, and you would leave the following Monday. In many cases, however, you will be asked to give a month or even longer. Where possible give your firm as long a notice period as possible as it may take several weeks, even months, to fill the vacancy with someone of comparable experience.

CHAPTER 6

Managing money

You will never be happy fending for yourself if you cannot manage your money. There is no doubt that some people are better at it than others, but if you are realistic about how much money you have coming in and how much you have to pay out, you should be able to stay solvent.

To begin with, write down all the money you have coming in – your grant, an allowance from your parents, wages or whatever. The amount for your wages must be net – that is, the amount you receive after all the deductions have been made for tax, national insurance and so on. It is a very different figure from the gross wage you will have been quoted when you applied for the job.

On another piece of paper write down all your outgoings for the same period. The list will cover accommodation and all the extras such as electricity, telephone, gas and so on. Include a figure for food and items such as shampoo, shoe polish, detergent, etc., plus incidental expenses such as newspapers and magazines, and build in an amount for buying clothes, too, even if you feel you will never be able to afford anything new ever again. (When you do buy clothes, bear in mind the cost of their unkeep: washing is infinitely cheaper than dry-cleaning.)

Travel is an expensive item, and should cover whatever it costs you to visit friends or go home for the weekend, as well as fares to and from work. If you run any form of transport, such as a bicycle or a car, allow for maintenance, insurance, road tax, fuel and so on, as applicable.

It is also important to build in some kind of savings if you possibly can, for holidays, tickets to a concert or a present for someone special. Even with the most basic lifestyle you will not want to go without one or two luxury items, but you need to plan for them, and keep them in proportion to what you can afford.

Once you have written down all your expenses you will most probably find that they add up to more than your income. Do not panic: it has happened to almost everyone at some time or other, even to millionaires.

The next thing to do is to go through each item and see how you can trim it down. On food, for example, buy your milk from a supermarket rather than from the milkman. Buy margarine instead of butter, use smaller eggs (you will not really notice the difference), buy own-brand food, having checked that it is cheaper than major brands, avoid buying pre-packed fruit and vegetables and cut out confectionery, which is expensive, fattening, and harmful to both your teeth and your complexion. As for fares, if they are a major problem, consider finding a flat nearer your job. Cut out smoking altogether.

On some other items you might find it easier to trim a little off each, or alternatively to cut out one expense completely. Perhaps you could do without something for a period of time: set yourself a goal, a date when you can review the situation – like the date when a pay rise is due, or your birthday, when you might expect to receive some money.

If you can get together a lump sum, however small, keep it for emergencies, in case you are made redundant, fall sick or some unexpected expense arises.

If you pay tax, put your money in a building society or bank deposit account where it can earn interest yet still be available at short notice if you need it. A post office investment account is worth considering too, as it pays good rates of interest without tax being deducted at source.

Most of your bills will come in a weekly or monthly cycle. If you are paid monthly, a monthly budget will be easier to follow. If you are paid weekly, work out your outgoings on a weekly basis. Do not forget that expenses such as birthdays and holidays, though less frequent, need to be allowed for.

ACCOMMODATION, TRAVEL AND HOUSEKEEPING

At the beginning you will almost certainly find that accommodation takes the biggest slice of your income. If you have a room of your own it will be more expensive than sharing, and while sharing bedrooms may not be ideal it may prove to be a worthwhile economy.

If you have a reasonable relationship with your landlord you might be able to barter some services in exchange for a cheaper rent: babysitting or cleaning, perhaps.

The cost of lighting and fuel may well be included in your rent, but if it is not and you are receiving bills every three months or so, you may be able to go on to a budget instalment plan whereby you pay a regular amount right through the year. Enquire at your local electricity or gas showrooms. Sometimes you may find the companies reluctant to offer a budget plan to anyone who lives in rented accommodation, for the obvious reason that tenants come and go so frequently. One alternative is to buy fuel stamps for gas and electricity at your local showrooms, to be set against the fuel bill. You can also buy stamps towards the cost of a TV license (enquire at your local post office). However, if you can organize your money so that you are saving towards all these bills in an interest-earning account (building society or bank deposit account, for example), you will actually be saving money as opposed to merely spreading the cost.

Travel and food will probably be the next most expensive items, depending on how near you live to your work.

You may be able to get an interest-free loan from your employers to buy a yearly season ticket or travel pass, which will save you a substantial amount of money. Alternatively, it might be worth your buying a bicycle for travelling to work, as long as you can leave it somewhere safe when you arrive. If you go by bus, try walking to the next fare stage, thereby saving yourself a few pence and giving yourself some exercise into the bargain.

To save money on leisure travel, consult your local travel agent. Some of the main forms of cheap travel for young people are listed in the reference section.

Food is a major item, but luckily the most nutritious foods tend to be among the cheaper ones (see Chapter 7). Many supermarkets have fresh-food counters, including fish, and by looking at what is on special offer each week you can make quite substantial savings. Buying for one person can be more expensive than buying for two or more, however, so if you share a flat it may be worth having a housekeeping kitty for buying basic foods such as butter, eggs, bacon, vegetables and so on, and items which are cheaper bought in larger sizes or quantities.

Make the most of money-off coupons in newspapers and magazines, and those that are pushed through the letter-box, but remember that they will only save you money if you wanted the product in the first place. You could try swopping coupons you do not want with friends or neighbours. Also, a few shops will cash the coupon regardless of whether you buy the product.

BANKING

Although almost 40 per cent of the adult population of Britain still does not have a current bank account, your money will certainly be easier to manage if you do.

Banks are very keen to get your business, and they provide attractive incentives to encourage new accounts. If you are a student ask your local banks what facilities they provide for students. If you have just started work your bank will help you organize your money. Most banks display various free booklets advertising their services, so go in and pick some up. Girobank's services are described on a leaflet available from post offices.

Before opening an account, take the trouble to shop around your local banks or ask your friends if there is a sympathetic bank manager in your area. A bank is only as good as the staff you have to deal with, and some managers are a good deal more helpful than others in understanding young people's problems.

Do not forget that very few banks are open at the weekend. Their regular hours are from 9.30 am to 3.30 pm Monday to Friday, and some branches of Barclays are also open on Saturday mornings, usually in major shopping centres.

The National Girobank is open for longer hours (9 am to 5.30 pm Monday to Friday and also Saturday mornings); cash can be paid into most post offices but cheques have to be sent post to the clearing house in the stamped addressed envelopes provided, so it takes a few days for them to be credited to your account. You can cash a cheque for up to £50 at almost any post office and can nominate one post office at which you may cash cheques of up to £100.

When you have decided which bank would suit you best, go to the enquiry desk and ask to open an account. You will be asked to fill in a form and supply the name of someone who will act as a referee. In some cases this can be your parents, or if not you can give the name of your employer or anyone who holds a bank account. You do not need a lot of money to open a bank account but obviously you should have some expectation of money to come.

There are many advantages in having a bank account. Your wages or grant can be paid in directly, and you will not need to carry so much cash about with you. Regular bills can be paid out of your account by standing order or direct debit.

A standing order is a way of paying the sort of bills you have every month, such as rent for accommodation, TV rental or a spread payment of gas or electricity bills. You tell the bank how much to pay and to whom, and the payments are made automatically. A direct debit arrangement is similar to a standing order, but works slightly differently. In this case you give your bank authority to accept charges by a third party against your account. This means that if, for instance, you pay a subscription by direct debit, when the price of the subscription increases the greater amount can be deducted from your account without your having to instruct the bank.

A cheque book together with a cheque card will make shopping easier. Banks can also help you to plan a budget account to spread the payment of bills, and can allow you overdraft facilities or a loan, both of which must of course be repaid with interest. They can also answer specific queries about your financial status, which is useful if you are applying for credit.

You can also apply for a cash card, which gives you access to the 24 hour cash dispensers now located outside many banks, but sometimes inside and therefore available only during normal banking hours. If you use a cash till take particular care to put your money away quickly and carefully to lessen the risk of being robbed.

Cheque cards, which guarantee the cheques you write up to a value of £50 and therefore make payment by cheque much simpler and easier, are not granted automatically, and it is difficult to get one unless you are 18 or over, have opened an account and have paid in your first month's wages or grant. Normally you can apply for a cheque card about six months after you have opened the account. In the meantime you may have to draw cash for everything you want to buy. Cheque cards are usually issued at the manager's discretion, so ask.

A Girobank cheque card has the same benefits as normal cheque cards in guaranteeing cheques up to £50, but again you usually have to wait six months for one after opening an account unless you already hold another bank's guarantee card (and again, you have to be 18 years old or over). If you do not have a cheque guarantee card Girobank will issue you with a standard 'identity card' to present at either of two named post offices where you wish to be able to cash cheques.

A credit card performs a quite different function from a cheque card. If it is issued by a bank, it will enable you to buy goods on credit up to a limit nominated by the bank and based on information you give the bank about your income. You have the option of paying back by instalments, in which case the interest charges are considerable, or to pay the total amount by the date given on the bill, which means you will have had an interest-free 'loan' for a few weeks on the amount payable.

Most large stores, with one or two notable exceptions, some garages and most hotels will accept payment by credit card, and having one certainly saves the bother and risk of carrying about large sums of cash or endlessly writing cheques. The disadvantage is of course the temptation to buy on impulse and run up bills without really considering whether you can afford to pay back the amount spent on the due dates.

To obtain a bank credit card, such as Access or Visa, or a charge card of the sort issued by American Express and Diner's Card (for which you pay both a substantial joining fee and an annual subscription), you must be 18 years old or over. If you want a bank credit card you will find the necessary application forms in any bank. If for any reason you are refused you might, if your parents agree, wish to apply for an attachment to your parents' card: this means that your parents will get the bills, and the application to the credit card company must come from them.

Some large stores issue their own credit cards, which are useful if you go regularly to one particular store to buy clothes or articles for your home. You can buy the goods on short-term credit and pay the whole amount at the end of the month. Sometimes stores offer budget-account terms, whereby you can pay back by instalments. Ask for details at the shop concerned but be prepared to supply references.

Bear in mind that 'plastic' does not cover all situations, and you must always keep a small amount of cash with you in case, for example, you need to take a cab when you miss the last bus home.

BORROWING MONEY

If you need to borrow money for an emergency, the best source is your parents or another relative or a friend, who may give you an interest-free loan. But before people part with their hard-earned cash in this way they will need to be convinced, primarily, that you have a good reason for asking for it and that they will get the money back. You are more likely to get sympathy and a hand-out if you need some money to repair your car than because you have seen a sheepskin coat at a bargain price.

It is worth asking your employer for a loan in some circumstances, particularly for a season ticket. Some large companies grant interest-free loans to their employees for this purpose, deducting the amount owing from the employee's salary cheque over the period covered. Find out from your personnel department, or your supervisor, if your company will do this for you.

If you have had a bank account for some time – at least a year – you may be able to get a loan from your bank. Make an appointment to see the manager, but before you see him, work out what you want to say; make a few notes if you think you may forget something. Then put your case pleasantly and straightforwardly.

The bank manager will want to know how much you want to borrow, and for how long, and will need some evidence that you have the means to pay it back. Before he sees you he will have checked on your account and your track record while you have been a customer.

Avoid at all costs going to a money-lender, who will charge you an extortionate rate of interest, and do not sign anything unless you understand it fully. You can always seek advice from your local Citizens' Advice Bureau (find the address in the library, or the telephone directory). Do not forget that they cannot help you much *after* you have signed.

For a loan from the Girobank fill in the relevant form, obtainable by writing to or telephoning Girobank. Ask about Flexiplan, too, which will give you credit up to 30 times an agreed monthly amount (ask for leaflet and a form).

HIRE PURCHASE

Though still a popular means of buying goods on credit, hire purchase is not a cheap option. Normally you pay a deposit, then instalments of equal amounts over a period of months or years, but it is important to remember that you are only the *hirer* of the goods until you have paid in full. You may not sell the goods until you have paid for them in full either. A credit sale is similar to hire purchase, but you own the goods right from the start. Make sure you understand agreements before you sign.

If you are buying hi-fi equipment or a car or some such item from someone privately, make sure the goods are not still subject to a hire-purchase agreement.

No shop or dealer will want to enter into a hire-purchase agreement with you if you are under 18 because the contract will be unenforceable by him.

THE TRUE COST OF CREDIT

Anyone who lends you money, unless it is a private arrangement between friends or relatives, is doing so in order to make money. By law, however, the agreement you sign must show the true rate of interest, generally called the Annual Percentage Rate of charge (APR). Everyone is obliged to work this out by the same set of rules, which means you can compare one form of credit with another, and the rate shown must include all the charges you have to pay to obtain the credit, including any administration fees.

The Office of Fair Trading has an excellent free leaflet called

There's More to Credit Than Just HP, available from your local Citizens' Advice Bureau or Trading Standards Department. Ask for the latter at your local council offices.

INCOME TAX AND NATIONAL INSURANCE

As soon as you start to earn a wage you may be liable for income tax, though you are allowed to earn a certain amount before tax is payable (this is known as the 'tax threshold').

When you start a job your employer will ask you if you have a P45, the tax record that you should take with you every time you leave employment. If it is your first job you will not have one, so he will give you a form to fill in; this will be sent to the company's tax office, who will send you another form to fill in and return, whereupon the tax office will assess your tax allowance and advise you and your employer of your code number. This number will tell your employer how much tax to deduct from your wages. In the meantime, your employer will have been deducting tax under an emergency code, which may well mean you have been paying more tax than necessary. Once the code number is issued it will enable this to be rectified, and you may receive a small refund.

National Insurance is deducted at source from your wages in the same way. This money pays for benefits such as sickness and unemployment as well as your retirement pension.

There are four different classes of National Insurance. Class I applies to people who work for an employer; Class II is for self-employed people; Class III covers voluntary contributions by people who may be neither employed nor self-employed but wish to maintain their benefit entitlement; Class IV is payable by self-employed people in addition to Class II contributions if they have earned over a certain amount of money in any one year.

HEALTH COSTS

Not all health requirements are provided 'free' by the National Health Service.

Unless you are under 16 you will probably have to pay for medical prescriptions. Under-16s should fill in the back of the prescription before they go to the chemist. Over-16s are sometimes eligible for free prescriptions on the grounds of low income, especially if still at school or college (ask at the DHSS office for leaflet P11).

You may be entitled to free spectacles if you are still at school or if you are on supplementary benefit (ask at the DHSS office for leaflet G11).

Dental treatment is free to under-18s and those still in full-time education, but if the latter is the case tell the dental receptionist you want free treatment when you make the appointment. Similarly if you are over 18 but have a very low income you may be entitled to free treatment (ask at the DHSS office for leaflet D11).

If you do not qualify for free treatment on age or other grounds you will have to pay for treatment each time, even on the NHS.

Contraceptives can be obtained free of charge from your local GP or local Family Planning Clinic, but you will have to undergo regular check-ups in order to obtain them.

MONEY PROBLEMS

If for some reason, such as unemployment, you get into real financial difficulties – you fall behind with the rent or with other monetary commitments – the important thing is to tell people, as soon as possible, rather than keeping it secret and allowing yourself to be overwhelmed by worry and shame. Tell your parents, or a close friend or relative whom you trust, your bank manager (who will help you plan your expenditure more carefully) and the people to whom you owe money. If the problem is indeed lack of paid employment, merely letting them know your need for a job might just result in one coming up through their own contacts. If things are grim, it is better to take a less-than-ideal job for a while just in order to stabilize your financial situation, and you can of course continue to look for the job you really want in the meantime.

Debt is a soul-destroying burden to carry, but just talking your problems over with somebody will help, and may produce some ideas that had not occurred to you.

CHAPTER 7

Staying healthy

Do you feel on top of the world? Full of energy and zest for life? If so, congratulations! You can put most of it down to good health. It is something we all take for granted until something goes wrong. But with a little knowledge and some sensible precautions most of us can stay healthy and full of well-being for most of our born days.

To maintain good health you must feel good about yourself, respect your body and know how to keep it in good condition. In return, a healthy body will enable you to be mentally alert, to keep going in times of intense activity, overcome stress quickly and remain in control of your life.

Keeping your body in good condition means eating well and taking exercise – to increase your stamina, keep you supple and build up your strength.

Most people have had some regular exercise forced upon them at school, whether they liked it or not, but tend to drop all forms of exercise on leaving. This is short-sighted, because some sort of exercise, not necessarily a sport, will improve your general well-being. So if you can build exercise into your regular routine it will stand you in good stead for the rest of your life.

Walking, running, swimming, aerobics classes, disco dancing and playing tennis are all excellent ways of taking exercise. The relative costs, time involved and location may have a bearing on which one you choose, but most people can at least find time for a brisk walk every day. Try to maintain the level of exercise so that it leaves you feeling breathless, though not to the extent that you feel the next gasp may be your last. If you have not exercised properly for some time go gently at first and build up gradually (there are plenty of books to read on the subject).

Yoga is excellent for keeping the body supple, and may lead you on to learning about meditation. Even at a basic level yoga will teach you valuable lessons in relaxation. Although you can pick it up from a book it is best to take classes with a teacher at first to learn the right way of going about it; then you can continue on your own.

If you have had a rotten day, or have been sitting at a desk for hours, slept badly or just feel tired, exercise can soon restore you to vitality again – ironically enough. In fact, experts insist that it is much better than soaking in a warm bath, as we were once advised.

Stamina is an important part of feeling good. It is not just about competing in a marathon; it is about carrying on with a project – writing an essay or finishing some office work – even when you feel exhausted. Stamina is the quality that enables you to finish the task or work far into the night, when you have to, without cracking up.

A brisk walk or a workout in a gym will do a lot more for flagging will-power than glucose sweets or endless cups of black coffee. And so will a sensible meal. A salad, piece of fruit or an omelette will all give you a slow release of energy to enable you to go on a little longer.

What we eat and the exercise we take are the key to health, and good health will help us withstand stress and adversity.

WE ARE WHAT WE EAT

This popular saying is very largely true, although there must be one provision in that what you have inherited from your parents also has a lot to do with it.

Apart from the genes that determine your body chemistry, your parents have largely been responsible for your eating patterns and attitudes to foods. From babyhood your mother will have decided on your behalf whether you should eat sweets, chips with everything or meat only once a week. If the eating pattern was a good one, so much the better, but if it left a lot to be desired you may find it difficult to break the pattern and improve the quality of what you eat, now that you have a choice.

If you are eating a varied diet you will not be going short of proteins, vitamins or minerals. The chances are you will be eating too much sugar, fat and carbohydrate. The Health Education Council says that on average we eat as much as twice the protein we need. Vitamin pills are rarely necessary: an average varied diet will provide sufficient vitamins. Unless you are a particularly fussy eater or have undertaken a crash diet (which is not recommended) you can forget about extra vitamins. The only item an average diet might lack is fibre, though with all the talk about it recently and the publicity given to high-fibre diets, it is hard to believe that some people are still not aware of its importance.

Views on nutrition have changed fairly radically over the last few years and what our parents thought was a good, balanced diet – plenty of meat, cheese, milk and eggs – has now been given the heave-ho by the medical pundits.

Everything in moderation is a wise course to follow, keeping fat and sugar to an absolute minimum.

Most people eat too much fatty food, which not only makes you fat but can lead to heart disease.

Buy wholemeal, not white bread, cut it more thickly and spread the fat more sparingly, or use a low-fat spread. Try to eat less cake, biscuits and pastry. Forget about chocolate and sweets except as a special treat.

Trim the fat from meat and remove the skin from chicken. Eat plenty of fish, preferably white fish such as haddock, cod or coley. Be wary of cheese: it can be extremely high in calories. Cheddar cheese, for example, has a 34 per cent fat content, though you can now buy a type of Cheddar and Cheshire cheese that has only half the fat. Edam and cottage cheese are also lower in calories. Forget about cream; eat yoghurt instead and buy lower-fat milk, such as skimmed milk.

The importance of fibre has been much publicized in recent years and it is easy and inexpensive to incorporate into your diet. Jacket potatoes, wholemeal bread, green leafy vegetables, pulses and high-fibre breakfast cereals are all simple ways to add to the fibre content of meals. Fibre not only provides roughage but helps to prevent bowel disorders such as piles and diverticulitis. Moreover, these fibre-filled meals will make you feel full sooner and thus help you to cut down on cakes and pastries.

The big bogey in the nutrition world is sugar, not only because it makes you fat but it can cause dental decay. The average British adult eats nearly a hundredweight of sugar a year. It is not an easy item to give up as many of the favourite foods we associate with the comforts of childhood, such as ice cream, cake, jellies and sweets, are horrifically high in sugar. (Commercial fruit yoghurts, as opposed to natural yoghurt, also contain a lot of sugar.)

If you take sugar in tea or coffee try cutting it down gradually. Aim to cut it out altogether in three or four months. Try not to resort to sugar substitutes. If you are getting used to a new taste, you might as well cut out any form of sweetener altogether. Ration your intake of sweets and cakes, and go easy on sugary drinks. Do not forget the hidden sugar in chutneys and savoury sauces, and that many canned goods, even vegetables and soups, contain sugar.

One problem is that if you are on your own there is a temptation to eat cakes and biscuits instead of something more nutritious. The same applies to chocolate. If you cannot cut it out completely, ration it to nibbles once or twice a week.

Eat more vegetables and fruit, especially raw. Raw vegetables may seem strange at first but try shredding or grating them and soon you will wonder how you could ever have cooked them. Potatoes baked in their jackets are rich in fibre and will fill you up without being too fattening. It is the butter you add that does the damage, so try topping them with plain yoghurt and freshly chopped herbs.

White fish is good for you, except when it is wrapped in batter and served with a pile of chips. Try some of the frozen packs – cod in parsley sauce or fish fingers. Dry-fry sprats when they are in season. They are very cheap and delicious sprinkled with lemon juice and served with brown bread.

Chicken without the skin is less fattening than other meats. Buying cooked portions will work out cheaper than baking a single portion in the oven, unless you are cooking other items at the same time. A leg of chicken sprinkled liberally with lemon juice then wrapped in foil and baked is extremely succulent eaten on its own or with a salad.

Use the cheaper cuts of meat to make a stew. Stewing or braising steak with root vegetables can be casseroled very simply even in a small oven, or cooked on a very low heat on the top of the stove. Minced beef is invaluable as there is no waste, and although some of the cheaper mince is fatty you can drain this off after cooking it in water in a pan. Use as little as you want, provided you have a refrigerator or other cool place to keep it. The liquid you have drained off will set, and if you remove the layer of fat on top you will have a transparent jelly which can be used as stock for your next casserole. Then the meat can form the base for a cottage pie, chilli con carne or spaghetti bolognese; try wholewheat spaghetti, or tagliatelle verdi, a delicious pasta blended with spinach.

Buying food for one can be expensive, especially if your plans are uncertain and you eat out unexpectedly, leaving your supper to go stale in the refrigerator, so keep a spare can or two, or some frozen foods, so that you do not have to waste perishable foods when your plans are uncertain.

Fortunately food shops are more aware now of how many people live on their own and consequently shop for one: small portions are on the increase (and some of the portions marked for two people are only substantial single portions).

Look out in the newspaper ads for supermarket special offers. Read the 'best buy' food reports to see what is on offer or good value because it is in season. Manufacturers are always having special weeks or months when their food is at a discount, so make the most of them, but do not be tempted to buy food you do not like or packs that are too large for you. Bacon pieces are very much cheaper than properly cut rashers, and you can often pick these up in a large supermarket. Use half the pack to make a flan and grill (do not fry) the remainder for supper to serve with a poached or boiled egg.

Markets are a good source of cheap food, though you have to watch closely for quality. Generally speaking, fresh food is very satisfactory as long as it is eaten quickly after purchase.

Try wandering round the stalls when the market is due to close – it is amazing what bargains you can pick up in food that will not keep.

Do not go shopping for food when you are hungry. It is fatal. Try to shop when you are not tired and can keep on your toes to spot a bargain. If you feel you might be tempted to buy food you do not really need, make a list before you set out and then stick to it.

'Own brands' are very often cheaper than the better-known names, but you need to check. Keep your eyes open to compare the weights on the cans and packs with the price before you decide.

Brown eggs can sometimes be more expensive than white ones though there is no nutritional difference. Choose medium-sized eggs: size 4 is a good all-round option.

EXERCISE

After leaving school, it is very easy to avoid taking exercise, but in the long run your studious avoidance will do you no good.

Regular exercise not only makes you feel better but is necessary to keep your heart and lungs in good condition and protect you against heart disease. It helps to keep you supple and increase your strength. It also helps to keep you slim and combat stress.

Although you do not need a medical check-up before you take up regular exercise (except if you have chest troubles, have ever had high blood pressure or heart disease, or have recently had back pain), it makes sense to start an exercise routine slowly and then build up. Do not take up vigorous games like squash until you know you are pretty fit. And do not expect miracles: it will take some time for regular exercise to make you feel fit. It is more important to do it regularly than have a great burn-out at the weekend, then forget about it for the rest of the week and thereby undo all the good work.

You can start your new regime simply by going for a walk.

Keep it fairly brisk and as far from city fumes as you can manage. Walk to work, or round to a friend's house instead of getting a bus, or, if that is not practical, at least walk to the first or second bus stop *after* the nearest. Wear sensible shoes. Walks can gradually turn into gentle jogs. Again, wear sensible clothes and track or training shoes. Walk, then run, then walk, taking it gently, then gradually increase your running time. The goal should be to feel breathless.

When you feel sufficiently fit, consider taking up some kind of regular sport. It will not only keep you healthy but acts as a wonderful safety-valve in giving you an outlet for stress, frustration or aggression, and will enable you to cut off from worries and problems for at least an hour or so, which in turn will lessen them.

The chart overleaf gives you a useful guide to most regular sports and what they can do for you. It shows sports in relation to the three Ss – strength, suppleness and stamina. The ideal combination of sports and activities promotes all three, though you may have to do more than one to fulfil all your needs. Try to make exercise an intrinsic part of your life, not something you take up between love-affairs or when you find yourself out of work.

ALCOHOL

Having a drink with friends is a lot of fun. It is a chance to relax and meet other people. The pub is a convenient and warm place to go on a cold evening, especially if you do not know many people in the area and cannot think what to do.

Sensible drinking is generally regarded as good for you. Sensible drinking, as defined by the Health Education Council, is two or three pints (or their equivalent) of beer two or three times a week. For women the equivalent is two or three standard drinks two or three times a week. A standard drink is defined as ½ pint ordinary beer or lager; single measure of spirits; a glass of wine; a small glass of sherry; a measure of vermouth or similar aperitif.

The ideal patterns quoted are meant to be distributed through the week. If you put all your drinking time into the weekend because you are studying the rest of the week, you will probably be affected by the alcohol more quickly. The measures quoted are standard pub measures, whereas the drinks people pour in their own home are very often a lot more generous. Take a note before you start drinking to see how they compare. (Standard measures may be larger in some areas, such as Northern Ireland and some parts of Scotland.) Homemade wine, lager or beer can

S-FACTOR SCORE

	Stamina	Suppleness	Strength
Badminton	★★	★★★	★★
Canoeing	★★★	★★	★★★
Climbing stairs	★★★	★	★★
Cricket	★	★★	★
Cycling (hard)	★★★★	★★	★★★
Dancing (ballroom)	★	★★★	★
Dancing (disco)	★★★	★★★★	★
Digging (garden)	★★★	★★	★★★★
Football	★★★	★★★	★★★
Golf	★	★★	★
Gymnastics	★★	★★★★	★★★
Hill walking	★★★	★	★★
Housework (moderate)	★	★★	★
Jogging	★★★★	★★	★★
Judo	★★	★★★★	★★
Mowing lawn by hand	★★	★	★★★
Rowing	★★★★	★★	★★★★
Sailing	★	★★	★★
Squash	★★★	★★★	★★
Swimming (hard)	★★★★	★★★★	★★★★
Tennis	★★	★★★	★★
Walking (briskly)	★★	★	★
Weightlifting	★	★	★★★★
Yoga	★	★★★★	★

    ★ *No real effect*
   ★★ *Beneficial effect*
  ★★★ *Very good effect*
★★★★ *Excellent effect*

(Reproduced by kind permission of the Health Education Council.)

be stronger than you would expect, so treat Aunt Mabel's Dandelion 1975 with caution.

Anyone who has just started drinking should not regard the above guide to sensible drinking as an immediate o.k. for similar alcoholic intake. The amounts quoted are for adults with some years of drinking experience behind them. When you first start to drink alcohol your tolerance level will be considerably lower;

in fact, one drink will make you feel 'fuzzy'. When you first start to drink alcohol you may not even like it very much; and there is no magic about it that makes you popular, handsome, pretty, witty or clever. If you do not find the taste to your liking stick to soft drinks. Never feel you have got to have a drink to be popular or socially accepted.

Even one drink will affect your ability to drive or work machinery. It can impair your judgement and make you slower to react. So although the legal limit is well above the amounts quoted, do not think that you are beyond danger if you keep below it.

On average, it takes an hour for your body to get rid of the alcohol in one standard drink, and longer if you are below average height. Tiredness and hunger will also affect how your body reacts.

If you have a drinking session at lunchtime then have some more alcohol in the evening you may still have the lunchtime's intake in your system. The same goes for a heavy evening's drinking: you could still have alcohol in your bloodstream when you set out for work the next morning, and you could still be over the legal limit for driving.

The legal limit for driving is approximately 2½ pints of beer or five single measures of spirits. If you drink that amount in an hour you will almost certainly be over the top, and will certainly be so if you are of lighter than average build or a woman. As it takes an hour to get rid of one standard drink you can work out the safety formula for yourself.

If you are afraid you might look silly in a group or at a party if you do not keep up with the drinking there are certain tactics you can use to avoid being conspicuously abstemious. Arrive at a party late. Drink sparkling mineral water (it is difficult for people to tell the difference between that and a mixer drink). Pace your drinks and make just one last a certain amount of time. Keep a full glass in your hand rather than one that is half empty, then people will not be so likely to come along and top you up. Work out in advance how many drinks you want to have, and find some way of remembering how many you have had. It is amazing how easily you can forget if you are having a good time.

When you feel you have had enough, either stop drinking altogether or get up and go home. Heavy drinking can lead to girls finding themselves in sexual trouble. Unwanted pregnancies and venereal disease are often started when people are extra vulnerable as a result of having had too much to drink. If you have food with your drink the alcohol will be absorbed more slowly and it will take longer to affect you. If you are going to a party and do not know whether or not there will be food, have a light meal before you go.

If you are giving a party yourself, do supply soft drinks as well as alcohol. Drinking alcohol makes you thirsty so it is always a good idea to have soft drinks, or mineral water. Do not push drinks on to people who say no: it does not make you a good host or hostess. Never slip a tot in someone's drink as a joke. If a guest has had too much, ply him with soft drinks or coffee, and if possible let him sleep it off until he has recovered. Do not let him drive home.

If you know you have had too much to drink yourself, do not drive. Leave the car if you have to and either walk home, get a lift from someone or order a cab. If you accept a lift make sure the driver is fit to drive.

Drinking with friends at home, in the pub or anywhere else should be fun. Do not underestimate the effect of alcohol, either in terms of legal limits for driving or in its ability to make you sad and depressed or happy and aggressive. It can change people's characters completely while the effect lasts. You are more likely to get involved in an argument, want to pick a fight, or feel witty and amusing when you are not, when you have had a drink. Remember that alcohol is a depressant, not a stimulant, as many people imagine.

Used wisely it is a pleasant ally, but used stupidly it can be your downfall.

SMOKING

Smoking can be a deadly habit, quite literally, so if you smoke try to beat it. Doctors tell us that on average people who die of disease caused by smoking lose ten to twenty years of their lives. Smoking leaves you wide open to heart attacks and lung disease as well as cancer. Women who smoke when they are pregnant run the risk of having a miscarriage or of producing a premature, underweight baby, who will have to struggle to survive.

So how do you give it up? The first step is obvious: you have to want to. If you want to stop enough, you will. It is as simple as that. Some people only manage to break the habit when their doctor scares them into it, but that can sometimes be too late and the damage may have already been done.

You may have been thinking for months or even a year or two that you would like to stop, so how *do* you kick the habit?

Having decided to stop, do not leave it too long before you take action. Some find it helpful to cut down for a week or two before they stop altogether, but it is a mistake to continue the cutting-down for too long or you may be content with smoking less instead of giving up.

Enlist the help of your family and friends. Most people, at least the friends worth having, will try to help and not try to trick you into starting again.

You may need to break certain routines, because smoking is a habit; it is often linked to certain times of day such as after a meal, when you are watching TV, or when you first get to work in the morning. By working out when these situations occur and knowing how to avoid them, you will help to further your resolve. After a meal do not sit at the table to chat. Get up and do something, even if it is only clearing the dishes. If you usually smoke when you are watching TV, either forfeit the TV or drink a cup of tea or give your fingers something else to do instead. Instead of lighting up when you get to work, reach for a cup of coffee.

Most people find they put on weight when they first give up smoking, but you can lose those extra pounds within a month or two if you are prepared to tackle the problem.

If you try to stop smoking when you are under stress you are less likely to succeed. Emotional problems or changing your job are bad situations in which to contemplate giving up smoking.

Having done it, however, you may find yourself unusually irritable for a week or so. The best way to tackle this is to admit it and ask your friends and family to put up with it in the knowledge that the irritability will be shortlived and they will all be benefiting from your effort in the long run.

Once you have stopped, you must stick at it. This may be difficult, and you may find yourself taking the odd puff, but if you do have a relapse it is not the end of the world. Simply resolve not to let it happen again.

Give yourself treats as a reward for each week you have kept your resolve. You will after all have saved some money, which you could spend on something you would not have been able to afford if you were still smoking. Take up a sport, perhaps one you have not tackled before: jogging, for example, now that your lungs are recovering from the damage you were doing them. Learn to relax in a different way: many people find they need to smoke when they are trying to unwind. And if you feel yourself getting het-up, instead of reaching for a cigarette start taking a few deep breaths and concentrate on breathing deeply and evenly.

It is difficult to say how long it will be before you do not fancy a cigarette. For some people it can be very soon, but others find it takes years. Do not ever presume that once you have stopped completely you can smoke occasionally without coming to any harm. If you get hooked again you will be back to square one.

Stopping smoking takes time and is not easy, but it is most certainly worth doing before you damage your body beyond repair.

MINOR ILLNESSES

Fortunately, most people with normal health are rarely ill, except for minor coughs and colds and the odd bout of vomiting. It is when you are feeling below par that you will be most aware of what independence means: you really *are* on your own, and there will be no one to 'look after' you when you feel ill.

You may feel a little apprehensive that if your condition worsens there will be no one to look after you. This fear will be stronger if you live entirely alone. It is a good idea to alert a friend, particularly one who lives nearby, and ask him or her to call in to check that you are o.k., or possibly to bring you in some shopping if you need it. If you have no one you can ask, you could ring your boss at work, to whom you will have reported that you were sick the first morning you failed to arrive for work, and ask him if he will telephone you once a day. If you live in a house with other people you could ask one of them just to put his or her head round the door occasionally. A phone call to your mother or other relative may just cheer you up a little, too.

Here are some basic tips on treating minor illnesses.

Influenza If you have 'flu you will be feeling pretty awful. You will feel weak and shivery and have an aching head, back and limbs. You will have a raised temperature, probably over 38°C (100°F).

There is no point in seeing a doctor as 'flu, caused by a virus, cannot be cured by antibiotics. Stay indoors and keep warm, and avoid other people as much as you can. Have plenty of cool drinks – water, fruit juice and/or milky drinks – and have light meals if you feel like eating. If you have lost your appetite, do not worry. If you feel feverish and your temperature is above 38°C, try taking soluble aspirin and rest in bed if you can.

If the 'flu persists for more than a few days or suddenly gets worse, consult a doctor.

Colds Colds are also caused by viruses, so an antibiotic is not necessary. Keep warm and well wrapped up when you do go out. You can buy various aids over the counter at a chemist's to ease any discomfort. A nasal decongestant will relieve a stuffy nose and so will throat tablets or lozenges if your throat is sore. Honey and lemon in hot water will sooth a cough; alternatively, buy a cough mixture. Soluble aspirin or Paracetamol tablets will help to ease a headache.

Vomiting Lie down and keep warm. Once your stomach has got rid of whatever has caused the trouble, you should be over the problem. Sip a little plain water: if you can keep it down, you should be back to normal very shortly. If not, stay lying down and repeat the process later.

Gastro-enteritis This is caused by food poisoning or a virus. The symptoms are violent sickness and diarrhoea. Do not take aspirin, which may irritate the lining of the stomach. Try to drink plain water to replace lost body fluids. If the symptoms last for more than a day, consult a doctor.

Diarrhoea is usually caused by a virus infection. Treat with a kaolin-and-morphine mixture. If it does not clear up in a few days, consult a doctor.

Fainting Fainting is not usually serious, but you will feel distinctly off-colour just before it happens. You will probably feel giddy and may come out in a cold sweat. Lie down or put your head between your knees. Breathe deeply and loosen any clothing around your neck.

Nose bleed Sit with your head forward and breathe through your mouth. Pinch the nostrils together with a handkerchief folded to make a pad. Bleeding should stop within 5–10 minutes. Do not sniff or blow your nose for some time afterwards or the bleeding may start again.

Cough and sore throat A warm drink of honey and lemon is soothing and there are various cough sweets and medicines on the market that will help the condition. A bad cough will keep you awake at night, so keep a drink by the bed.

Do not forget that some illnesses, such as 'flu, can leave you feeling mildly depressed, so when you are on the mend aim to give yourself a treat.

The minor illnesses described above usually clear up by themselves, but if you develop any complications, or you seem to be getting worse instead of better, you should see your doctor.

It is also sensible to consult a doctor if you start to lose weight when you are not on a slimming diet; if you feel permanently listless and tired even after a regular good night's sleep and without any obvious stress; if you are having any unusual vaginal discharge (unlike the normal clear discharge); if you think you have VD (see below) or are worried that you might have any other disease.

SEXUALLY TRANSMITTED DISEASES

Sexually transmitted diseases are on the increase. Our attitudes to sex have changed dramatically over the last twenty or thirty years and as a result such diseases have become much more common.

Casual sex is responsible for a great deal of it, so if you or your sex partner suffer from any of the following symptoms you should seek advice without delay: (1) a persistent itching or soreness in the vagina, penis or anus; (2) a sore lump or rash on the genital area, anus or in the mouth; (3) a desire to pass water more frequently, and some discomfort whilst doing so.

As there are more than twenty-five germs that can be transmitted sexually there is no way you can treat yourself or even know exactly what your problem is.

The best step to take is to visit a special clinic or department of genito-urinary medicine, where there will be specialized staff and equipment to deal with such problems. The staff are tactful, understanding and quite matter-of-fact about sexual diseases, so you will not be made to feel embarrassed or that you are under censure. You can find the address of the nearest clinic in notices displayed in public lavatories, or in the telephone directory under 'Venereal disease'.

At the clinic it is essential that you are honest and tell the whole story. By covering up for someone or being evasive in your answers to questions you will delay your own treatment and help for other people who may need it too.

The doctor will want to know what symptoms you have, and how long you have had them; what sex partners you have had over the last three months and whether you can track them down; if you have had anal contact or oral genital contact. Your answers to his questions about your sex activities will help him make a diagnosis; all kinds of sexual activity, homosexual as well as heterosexual, can produce symptoms. He will also want to know whether you are allergic to any drugs.

You will be asked to undress and will be given an examination which will include your genital area. A blood test and a sample of urine will be taken.

You will not necessarily find any visible symptoms to tell you whether you are infected. Some men and women have no symptoms at all. So if you suspect or have been told that you have had sex with an infected person, you should check up by visiting the local clinic.

If it seems likely that you have a sexually transmitted disease, you must not have any sexual activity while you are being treated nor until you are declared free from infection.

The most common forms of venereal disease are gonorrhoea, syphilis, non-specific urethritis (NSU), candida (thrush), trichomoniasis, herpes, pubic lice and genital warts.

HEAD LICE
Head lice can afflict anyone. They are not fussy. They like clean hair just as well as less clean, and whether it is curly or straight it is all the same to lice.

If you come in close contact with someone already infected you will find they will transfer to you too.

It is a good idea to check your own hair every now and again by looking in the mirror, or get a friend to do it for you. If your scalp feels itchy, have a very close inspection.

Head lice are small, greyish insects and they tend to stay close to the scalp. They feed by biting the scalp and sucking blood. The eggs are oval in shape and stick to individual hairs.

You cannot mistake dandruff for head lice as the dandruff flakes are dull and loose. Louse eggs are shiny and stay firmly attached to the hair.

If you find you have been infected ask your chemist for a special lotion. Ordinary shampoo does not kill the lice or their eggs.

Normally the treatment will be to rub the lotion into the hair and scalp and leave it to dry naturally. After about 12 hours the hair can be shampooed in the usual way. It is best to let anyone you are sharing a flat or room with know you have head lice. It may be embarrassing but unless they know they may become infected too. Do not borrow anyone's brush and comb and make sure that yours are washed very thoroughly.

Head lice can happen to anyone, so do not worry about what the chemist will think. He will have seen it all before.

STRESS
Stress affects people of all ages, not just high-powered executives or people suffering from bereavement or the aftermath of divorce. Anyone leaving home for the first time or students studying for examinations are under extreme and very complicated pressures.

Life would be extremely boring without the ups and downs caused by various stresses in our daily pattern. It is when the patterns are too extreme and we cannot naturally cope with all the changes that we have cause to worry. A certain amount of anxiety is good for us. It can sharpen our reactions, and it gets jobs done, gives us the incentive to study hard for examinations or solve problems at work. But when outside influences, be they family problems, work, housing difficulties or money pressures, go beyond your ability to cope you will be under considerable stress.

This may make you irritable, impatient, permanently tired and unable to sleep, not to mention depressed and unable to concentrate. Little tasks or problems you would normally take in your stride seem to assume gigantic proportions.

There is nothing new about stress. It has always been there, but modern living is more complicated than it has been at any other time in history. We have so many different things to do, often all at the same time, and we have more choice, which leads to different kinds of pressure.

People most likely to suffer from stress are often similar in personality. They may be ambitious, impatient and competitive.

If you feel that the stress is becoming more than you can cope with, try to examine the reasons for your feelings. What puts you under pressure? Could it be not having a job, arguments with your parents, a feeling that you may be losing your boyfriend, overwork? Some pressures are self-inflicted, of course. If you spent your rent money on a new pair of shoes and have to hide from the landlord, you have brought it on yourself. If you always get up at the last minute and are constantly late for work so that your boss complains, you know only too well what you can do to remove that aggravation.

It may help if you do one job at a time instead of trying to do everything at once and achieving little or nothing.

Take some time off for exercise: a competitive sport may be just what you need. A game of squash, for example, leaves you no time for any other thoughts; sailing, too, is a great relaxer. Many people have found yoga brings them the chance to unwind and recharge their batteries.

Wind down before you go to bed at night. Sit and relax by watching TV or reading a book. Do not dash around right up to the last minute until you keel over exhausted; take time to wind down, or you will find it difficult to sleep even though you are very tired. Funnily enough, milky drinks *do* seem to help you sleep (but not coffee).

If after trying to eliminate stress over several months you find that the situation has not improved, it may be time to sit down and examine your lifestyle seriously. Are you really doing what you want to be doing? Do you hate your job, or live in a big city in a noisy street when you really want to live in a small town or a quieter environment? Should you leave your job and go off and do something completely different?

Do you have any friends to whom you can really talk? Is the

fact that you have to bottle everything up aggravating the condition? If you really do not have anyone you can confide in, talk to the Samaritans. They will listen to you sympathetically and try to help you sort out your problems. The telephone lines are always manned, 24 hours a day, and you will find the number in your local telephone directory.

If overwork is your problem, ask youself whether all this effort is leading to a worthwhile goal. If the stress of overwork is to be shortlived, that is fine, but if maintaining your job and striving for promotion is going to make such stress a permanent part of your lifestyle you must question whether the work is really right for you.

Do not expect to be able to answer such important questions overnight. You may have to think about your situation over several months and take even longer to decide what to do about it. But even if, after all, you decide to do nothing and continue your lifestyle as it is, you will have made important discoveries about your inner motives and feelings which will stand you in good stead for the future.

DRUGS

You do not need anyone to tell you that taking drugs, other than those prescribed by your doctor, is very dangerous.

It is easy to start, especially when it seems fun and fashionable and lots of your friends, or perhaps even trendy parents, are doing the same.

The problem is that it is extremely easy to become hooked, and no one knows exactly how drugs will affect you as they have different effects on different people.

People take drugs for various reasons. The most common are that they wish to be accepted by their friends and to feel part of a group, that they want to dispel anxiety and temporarily remove any stigma of failure, or to relieve boredom (taking drugs for 'kicks').

It is against the law to possess certain 'controlled' drugs such as heroin or cannabis unless they have been obtained on prescription. Police have powers to search anyone they think might be in possession of these, including their homes and vehicles.

It is possible that you will never come up against people who take drugs; up to a point the likelihood will depend on where you live, the sort of job you do and, most of all, the sort of people you have as friends.

Do not believe anyone who tells you that drug-taking cannot harm you or that you will not become addicted if you try them.

Only experts can tell you the truth about drugs, and people who are already using them are likely to be unreliable informants. Anyone who has undergone treatment to cure drug addiction will, however, tell you that the experience is unpleasant in the extreme.

CHAPTER 8

Making friends

Once the excitement of finding a job and settling in a new home has passed, you will have time and opportunity to meet people and make friends.

Living away from home can be a lonely experience at the beginning and you must expect to feel rather strange and isolated even when you are apparently surrounded by people.

This is particularly so if you are not used to city life or have always had plenty of personal space, such as your own room at home, a family garden or country lanes and fields to walk in.

One of the first things you will notice about the city is that people seem to be in a perpetual hurry, uninterested in people around them and often brusque. The style of life in a big town inevitably leads to a quicker pace, which you will acquire yourself given time. But it is important to find people you can chat to so that you can gradually build up your own network of acquaintances and friends.

The people you live with will be the first support group you find, which is why it is so important to decide that you will like them. It helps a lot to have someone to talk to when you come home from work and want to talk about your day, or to cheer you up when you have problems, or listen when you have an amusing incident to recount.

Do not hesitate to make contacts with people you used to know who now live in the city. Before you leave home collect phone numbers from your friends and your parents. Their friends will probably ask you to a meal or two, which will make a change from cooking for yourself. Most people are responsive to a phone call from someone who has just arrived in a new district. Overseas visitors make excellent use of this kind of network to meet people who are resident, as opposed to other tourists.

If you have not done so already, start an address book listing all the names, addresses and phone numbers you can think of. Carry it around with you whenever possible and keep filling it up regularly. It will always be the address you did not write down that you will really need one day.

Neighbours can sometimes turn into friends, or at least allies, if you approach them diplomatically. They will be glad to tell you where to find the nearest launderette, the Indian takeaway, or when the last bus goes, and they will know better than you what is going on locally. You may like them enough to ask them in for a coffee, but over-friendly neighbours can become a nuisance, so do not overdo the hospitality, and do not be too inquisitive about them or their affairs or you may find them backing off.

The next group of people who will provide you with some kind of relationship is the people with whom you work. Be cautious. A certain office etiquette prevails, and you should avoid socializing with your boss or others in positions considerably above yours, with any married romeos or with customers and clients.

Mixing socially with your boss or with other people in higher positions will cause problems, not least with your own contemporaries who will regard your association as 'crawling' and be deeply suspicious. There will also be difficulties if or when the friendship fades, if you get to know too much about each other's private lives or if, on closer investigation, you find you are not compatible.

Fraternizing with married men is nearly always doomed to disaster. No matter what you may be told, the majority of men do not leave their wives and children for someone they meet through work. If you get emotionally involved you can waste years of your life hanging on hoping. Your entanglement will stop you meeting other people who can offer a genuine friendship, and once the affair ends you will find it extremely difficult to carry on as if it never happened, which usually means that one or other of you will have to leave the company or take a job that would make further contact unlikely.

Customers or clients are best avoided, too, if the development of a close friendship or its decline could directly affect the business relationship.

What is useful about making friends in the office is that you can spend time with them over lunch or a drink after work and get to know more about the town or city where you work. They can tell you about the cafés and pubs nearby, the local shops and maybe exercise classes you could attend after work. Talking to your colleagues will also give you an insight into the office politics.

When you first look around to develop a social life, do not go out with the fixed desire to meet only the opposite sex. You need time to settle down in your new environment and put down a few roots. This is more easily done if you set out to make friends rather than to meet the partner of your dreams. In any case, by spreading your net wider you are more likely to meet interesting people of both sexes who will further your choice.

Even if you do meet someone to whom you are strongly attracted, do not fall straight into his arms. Though he may seem to be everything you ever dreamed of your judgement may be clouded while you get into your new social stride. After all, in striking out on your own you are bound to change in both your ambitions and your attitudes. Take any friendship slowly, and do not narrow your social life by going out with one person to the exclusion of all others. Even if you have, after all, found a permanent partner, you will still need other friends of both sexes.

Not all jobs produce a chance to make friends and nor do all bedsits or flat-shares. You will need to go elsewhere to make contacts: no one is going to knock on your door and become a friend if you stay at home every night eating Chinese takeaways and watching TV.

Unlikely places can make good starting points. The local launderette has often proved a splendid location for forming friendships. So can the supermarket when you are late-night shopping. Be prepared to initiate a conversation rather than waiting for someone else to speak first. Not all lonely people or potential friends will be your own age. If you start talking to a pensioner you may be pleasantly surprised; the harrassed mother with two small children may be only too pleased to talk to an adult for a change.

Do not stop to think up any earth-shattering remarks: 'What time does this store close?', 'Did you see if they have any fresh milk?' or 'I often wanted to try brown rice but I don't know how to cook it' can be sufficient to stimulate a chat. Try to look friendly. The person with an open, approachable face will make friends far more quickly than the raving beauty with a sulky pout. Do not be too put off if your first overtures come to nothing and do not let it stop you trying again.

One of the most difficult things to do is to go to places on your own when everyone else seems to be in couples. It can be daunting, especially if you feel unsure of yourself or homesick or unhappy for any reason However, if you look more closely you will soon find that there are people like you who have come on their own, or even if they have come with someone else are sufficiently detached from them to welcome the chance to talk to someone different.

You can make new friends in the park when you are out for a

walk. It is an ideal place not only to get fresh air but also to see a good cross-section of the community, ranging from dog-owners exercising their pets to children playing, jogging enthusiasts and people playing tennis or buying ice cream.

If you are a dog-lover, of course, you should have no problems. There is not an owner alive who will not stop to talk about his or her pet or discuss yours with you. Very often dogs are exercised at the same time each day, so it does not take too long to be on conversational terms. Looking at gardens that are open to the public is another way of meeting others with horticultural interests; an amble through a good garden centre will do almost as well. Even if you have no garden you can always hover over the pot plants and ask advice about the plants if anyone who seems knowledgeable comes into view.

Art galleries and museums are other places to meet people. Even if you do not strike up a conversation while gazing at a masterpiece you may still find someone to chat to over a cup of coffee in the coffee-shop.

An evening job as a waitress or behind the bar of a pub will certainly get you into the business of meeting others, though you may have to be discriminating about how you react to any friendship offered. Think hard before accepting lifts home from customers, however tempted you may be when it is raining or it is very late. Many employers will send late staff home in a mini cab or at least ensure you have adequate transport home.

Do not get too friendly too fast when you have no obvious means of discovering more about the background of someone you have met. Find out what you can about him before you start dating, and certainly before you tell him where you live or invite him back home.

Your sport or hobby could be a splendid passport to meeting people, with the added bonus that you will immediately have something in common. Evening classes are a good starting point. Most local authorities run a wide variety of classes you can join and there is bound to be one that suits you. If you are going more from a desire to make friends than to learn something, choose a class that has a coffee-break during the evening or is one where you can participate and talk at the same time – like car maintenance, for instance.

See what is on at the local sports centre and join a badminton or a self-defence class. Learn-to-swim classes for adults are often held in local baths, so if you cannot swim this could be a good chance to learn and meet local people at the same time. Sports clubs can be fun but are often expensive to join, and there may be a waiting list. It may take some time for you to get to know anyone. Some clubs are undeniably cliquey, but do not let that put you off because if there is some specially tight-knit group at the core you can guarantee that you will not be the only person excluded; look for others hovering around the edge and chat to them instead.

If sports do not appeal you could consider joining the local branch of the political party of your choice and becoming involved in its activities. All local parties need voluntary helpers and so do local pressure groups and groups that support charities. There is a wealth of activity going on behind the scenes, whether it is for a conservation society or a youth group raising funds for a special project. They all need people who can spare time and want to get together to do something worthwhile.

Helping other people less fortunate than yourself is another way to make friends. Many of the big charities have support groups at local level and they welcome helpers who are prepared to raise funds, help at meetings or assist in organizing outings. Whether their interest is in helping with the mentally handicapped or raising funds for the local PDSA, people who may have joined in rather hesitantly often wake up to the fact that they are also having fun. Local groups that need this type of help often have posters on display in the local library. You may also see notices asking for someone to help a child, or an adult, with reading problems, or someone to do shopping for or visit an elderly person.

Sometimes animal rescue centres need voluntary help. Again, they often put a card on the noticeboard at the library. Failing that, your local Citizens' Advice Bureau will be able to help put you in touch with a group needing assistance.

You can forget the old image of plain maiden ladies with stout flat shoes dispensing largesse in the afternoons. Today's volunteers are widely assorted but include young and enthusiastic, lively and intelligent men and women who are prepared to do something positive where the need arises.

The most important attribute, after wanting to help, is to be reliable. If you offer assistance it is vital that you turn up when you say you will, and on time. If, for example, you are scheduled to take a mentally handicapped person to a dental appointment or to serve tea in an old people's home, it is no good turning up late.

Do not harbour too rosy a view about what you will find. Old people are just like everybody else – sometimes moody and difficult and sometimes delightful. Similarly, dogs that have been ill-treated can bite and other helpers can sometimes be bossy. You just have to take the rough with the smooth.

Hospital volunteer work will be pretty basic: pushing trolleys of magazines or arranging patients' flowers or taking the telephone to them – even washing-up on occasion. People usually volunteer for a time, for whatever their reasons, and then move on, and most organizations accept this. Sometimes, if you are unemployed or between jobs, you can undertake a greater commitment for a while (see pages 120–2).

SOLO SURVIVAL
When you find yourself on your own, for whatever reason, do not stay in and watch TV when you would really rather be out and about. Try eating out on your own, perhaps in a wine bar that serves food or the local Indian restaurant or an upmarket serve-yourself. Get accustomed to eating alone and you will soon be reassured to discover that no one is any more interested in you than any other diners.

If you find going to the cinema or a concert alone rather daunting, look around for some of the first-class amateur shows that abound. There may be a classical concert in a local church; amateur theatre groups produce excellent plays and for some reason it is easier to attend this sort of show on your own. The atmosphere is usually less formal, even if the surroundings are sometimes grim. If you like what you see sufficiently, you may want to join the group yourself.

Going to a party on your own is easier than you might think. Take care with your dress, so that whatever you are wearing looks good and helps to boost your ego. Do not arrive too late, when everyone will have settled into groups. By arriving fairly early you may be able to organize your own. If you end up with a natural break during the evening when you find you are alone either go to the loo or ask your host or hostess whether you can help. Look to see if anyone elderly has been invited – they may be glad of someone to talk to, and so will any children if they are just tagging along. Not only will you almost certainly find them interesting but it will give you a breather before you re-launch yourself into the throng. Try to look as if you are having a good time. The saying 'smile and someone will smile back' really is true.

Go steady with the drink (see page 81). Avoid falling back on alcohol to give you a temporary boost. Clutch a drink by all means, but keep your glass topped up to prevent people plying you with more.

Give the party time to develop, but if you find you are not enjoying yourself, say, by the time the food has been served, or after a couple of hours, make your excuses and leave. What will most likely happen, though, is that by that time you will be having such a good time that you will have forgotten you came on your own.

MAKING FRIENDS OUT OF ACQUAINTANCES
Meeting people is one matter. Turning them into friends is another. Friendships are like pot plants: they need regular attention and nourishment to grow.

All friends start off as acquaintances. Usually it takes time for them to develop into friends. Instant friendships rarely happen, especially friendships that may last a lifetime.

Most of us only make a clutch of really close friends. It is impossible to keep a close friendship going with a large number of people.

The more acquaintances you make the greater the likelihood there is of one of them becoming a close friend. Friends do not have to come from exactly the same background or be the same age as you are. You may discover that you have a close rapport with someone of completely different origins or of another age-group.

People often form deep friendships based on shared experiences. That is why holidays, even a weekend hostelling or learning a craft, can sometimes turn an acquaintance into a friend.

Close friendship means commitment. Would you be willing to drop everything and go to your friend's aid if disaster struck? Would you listen to his or her problems on the telephone if you had just started eating a meal? Can you really like your friend for what he or she is, warts and all? Will you support her even when you disagree with her? Would you ever betray a confidence, or criticize your friend in the presence of others?

Once you have made a friendship, do not take it for granted. You cannot ignore friends for months while you engage in a hectic love-affair and then expect them to prop you up when it goes wrong. Regular contact is the simplest way to keep friends. Even if you cannot see them you can always phone or write a letter. You could even send tapes of news and gossip. Be ready to give, not only in material ways such as lending an interesting book or an outfit for a wedding but in terms of your time, for listening.

Friends can be of either sex. Not every contact between a man and a woman has to have a sexual or romantic undertone or motive. It can be very rewarding to have a friend of the opposite sex without sex playing any part in the relationship. The basis of any true friendship is mutual respect, loyalty and commitment.

Do not be in any rush to pair off. Some of the happiest times you will ever have will probably be spent with a small mixed group of people you like – out for the day, on holiday, sharing some other social activity, or perhaps engaged on a work project. Enjoy these experiences for what they are – easy, uncomplicated relationships through which you will come to know other human beings better and enjoy their company even more.

CHAPTER 9

Sex matters

Although you may find it hard to believe, your parents will have influenced your attitude to sex. If they found it easy to display their love for each other and for you during your childhood, you yourself will have absorbed a similar pattern of behaviour. If they were more rigid in their attitudes, embarrassed or even disapproving about sex, you may have this attitude yourself or feel extremely uneasy and anxious about it. The biggest influence in your views about sex will probably be your own friends. You will most likely have discussed with friends matters relating to sex from an early age – you will have been given wrong information by them, heard exaggerated and misleading stories, and also absorbed some of their attitudes.

What you read in newspapers or magazines and hear discussed on television has an enormous influence, and some of this can be harmful because it can raise your expectations beyond a reasonable level.

Regardless of what you see on television, in films and in magazines, even the most confident and beautiful people have fears and anxieties, just as you have. People have worried about the same topics for generations: whether their breasts are too small; whether their penis is too small; whether they will be able to have satisfactory sex or find a loving lifelong partner. The size and shape of parts of the body have very little to do with your ability to make people happy or to satisfy them sexually, in just the same way that you do not need to be a great beauty to be popular or to conform to one precise size and shape to be considered attractive.

If you can sit down with your mother or father and have a frank talk about sex and relationships you are fortunate indeed. It will give you a chance to discuss with someone of experience and a certain amount of worldliness your own feelings and self-doubts, and it will reinforce, perhaps improve, your own close relationship with those who love you and on whom you have relied all your life. Even if you feel you cannot discuss such matters with your parents you may find you have someone else you can talk to – a friend's parents, an older friend of your own, a teacher, doctor or perhaps someone at a club you attend.

Girls as well as boys boast about their sex lives but very often they are boasting to cover up their own fears and anxieties. Do not think that you have to do what everyone else appears to be doing: in any case, their activities may be mostly in their imagination. If you do not want to have sex with a particular person, or even to contemplate having sex with anyone, you should stick to your guns and do what you feel is right for you. Even if your friends tease you, they will soon get tired of doing so if they see it does not upset you or cause you to change your mind.

Choice is the name of the game today – and you should no more react to pressure concerning sexual relations than you would about changing jobs or flats.

It is quite easy when you are inexperienced to confuse sex with love. Boys can quite easily have sex with a girl they care little about, but a girl will feel far more committed to her sexual partner. Those magic words 'I love you' mean different things to different people. For a man it may mean 'I want to have sex with you', and for a girl it may mean 'I want to spend the rest of my life with you'. So it is easy to see that there can be much confusion.

Very often, in the complicated process of growing up, girls find they are attracted to girls, and boys to their own sex. This very often passes, but not always. If you feel permanently attracted to people of your own sex you could be a homosexual. When you first discover these feelings you may feel frightened, as you will feel cut off from so many of your friends. You will need to talk to experienced counsellors who can help you sort out your attitudes and give advice. If you have no one you feel you can confide in, contact the Samaritans, whose phone lines are open 24 hours a day. Counsellors will be happy to listen and offer advice or put you in touch with more experienced counsellors. The local number for the Samaritans will be in the telephone directory.

If your feelings for people of the same sex persist and you want to meet more like-minded people you can get in touch with a local gay group. Gay groups exist in most towns. Sometimes they are publicized in the classified advertisements in the newspaper or local free-sheet. If you cannot find a club locally write to *Gay News*, the newspaper for homosexual men and women, or telephone the Gay Switchboard, which has a 24-hour telephone advisory service not only in London but also in other major towns which will tell you about local events for gays. Look in the telephone directory under Gay Switchboard. It also runs a telephone counselling service, and can put you in touch with sympathetic doctors and solicitors or clergymen. Lesbian Line operates a similar service for women.

Your sexual standards are your own, and it is essential to be guided by what you feel is right and not to be too influenced by other people's attitudes. If you feel your friends are moving ahead faster than you want to yourself, be prepared to pull back or go out with them less often.

When you do meet someone who becomes more than just a good friend, try to keep your relationship honest. Do not play games: playing hard-to-get one minute then being a tease the next can have consequences for both of you that can be harmful. If one of you is genuinely in love but not the other, the situation will be quite painful enough without the other party pretending things he or she does not feel.

Do not neglect all your other friends now that you have found a partner to love. It is easy to do but you need to sustain relationships with existing friends – relationships which are under no emotional or sexual pressures. Try, too, to keep up your studies or hobbies so that you will have plenty of other interests if by any chance your romance goes awry.

No one can be all things to all people, so do not expect your new partner to be perfect or to supply all your physical and emotional needs. Blinding yourself to other people's faults is not love, and you will be storing up trouble for the future if you pretend to yourself that everything is perfect when you know in your heart that it is not. True love is based on accepting people for what they really are, not for what you would like them to be. Beware the friend who sets out to change you; the boyfriend who persuades a girl to dye her hair blonde when she liked it as it was, or buys all her clothes for her and constantly tries to change her personality, is more in love with an image than with the real person and both of them will eventually be disappointed.

To find a successful long-term relationship you will need to look for someone who likes you as you are, and has similar standards and attitudes to your own. We all know people for whom quite the opposite appears to be true. They are attracted to people of different cultures or standards, and appear, at least on the surface, to be extremely happy. This may well be so: mercifully, we are all different. But normally you have a greater chance of a successful relationship with someone whose ideas and attitudes are similar to your own.

Do not let a relationship that has gone sour drag on. So often people carry on seeing each other not because they really want to, but because they wonder what else they would do on a Friday night, or where they would go if they could not go and see all their mutual friends down at the pub. All relationships have their ups and downs, but sometimes they have so obviously come to a natural end, on one person's part if not on both, that severing the connection is the only sensible thing to do.

Saying goodbye to someone you have spent some time with, even loved, is difficult and painful. If your feelings have changed you will feel embarrassed and sad that you have to let go. To the person who still hankers after trying again to make a go of it, it can be devastating. There is no point in prolonging the agony, or agreeing to see each other less often. That is only postponing the moment of parting. 'I'm sorry, but I don't think we should see each other any more after tonight,' is brutally direct but better than sidling out of the relationship so that the other person is not quite sure where he or she stands.

Sex is a powerful force and it is possible to be strongly attracted sexually to someone with whom you have little in common, then, once you think about it, do not even like very much. Liking a person, especially if you are considering marriage, is extremely important, as it is the emotion that is most likely to survive long-term. Respecting other people's views is important too, as well as being at ease in their company and feeling comfortable when you are with their friends and they with yours.

Whatever your personal views about having sex and with whom, sooner or later you will need to get advice about contraception. It is irresponsible in the extreme and very foolhardy to have sexual intercourse without taking precautions.

Contrary to some myths that percolate, it is possible to conceive the first time you have sex. You can also conceive whether you have sex lying down or standing up, and it is also possible to become pregnant when the penis does not directly enter the vagina.

Family Planning Clinics offer contraceptive advice, counselling and practical help, and so do the Brook Advisory Centres in London and many other major cities, particularly to young people. Various methods of contraception are available. Your clinic or doctor will advise which is best for you. Some methods are more reliable than others, so weigh up the options carefully before you decide. Your own GP may be able to help if he or she gives family planning advice. Contraception is free.

In an emergency the morning-after pill can be taken, within

three days (72 hours) of intercourse, so if you have had unprotected sex you could, by acting quickly, prevent a pregnancy.

IF YOU THINK YOU ARE PREGNANT

If you have had sex without taking adequate precautions, there is a strong chance that you will become pregnant. If your period is 14 days late you should seek advice without delay. Go to the Family Planning Clinic, the Brook Advisory Centre or your local GP, who will give you a free pregnancy test.

Do-it-yourself pregnancy tests are less reliable. If the test pronounces you pregnant you almost certainly are, but if you are not, according to the kit, check again in a week's time.

Old wives' tales that drinking gin and taking very hot baths will abort the pregnancy are totally untrue.

At the clinic you can have a test that will give you the result immediately. Then you can talk to a counsellor about whether you want to go ahead with the pregnancy or wish to be referred for an abortion. If you wish to terminate your pregnancy, your first visit should be to your local GP, who may or may not be sympathetic.

If you receive no help from that quarter you should contact one of the Pregnancy Advisory Services which can be found in most big cities. Look for the address and phone number in the phone book. If it is agreed that you should have an abortion you will be given one free under the NHS, or you can attend one of the private clinics.

Conditions relating to abortion vary very much from one part of the country to another, and it is important to get advice fast.

Although you must move quickly if you are considering a termination of pregnancy, do stop to consider the possibilities open to you, and remember that the father-to-be is also involved. Whether or not he accepts his responsibilities will vary depending on his maturity, personality and a host of other factors. Before you do anything, try to pluck up courage and talk to your parents. You may well find them far more supportive than you had dared to hope.

Consider all the avenues open to you – marrying the father, bringing the baby up as a single parent, or having the baby adopted. Such a major decision taken in a state of shock will be more than you can handle on your own, so it is essential that you talk to someone close to you and who really cares about you, as well as a counsellor who can give you factual advice.

Having an abortion is a very serious step to take, and although it may seem to be the only way open to you, it may cause you to suffer great guilt and unhappiness in the future. If you have moral doubts that this is the right step for you, or if you feel you are under undue pressure from, say, your parents or your boyfriend to have an abortion, contact an association such as Life (Save the Unborn Child Association), of which there are 250 groups throughout Britain.

Other societies that can help are the Catholic Child Welfare Council, in Oxford, the National Council for One-Parent Families, in London, and Lifeline, in London and elsewhere.

If you decide to go ahead with the pregnancy, you will need to know about the welfare benefits available to you. Write for the booklet *Single and Pregnant* (70p), from the National Council for One-Parent Families.

SEXUAL ASSAULTS AND RAPE

'Rape' is an emotive word, and even today the public reaction is not always supportive of women who have undergone such a horrific experience.

Some people still think that only women who have 'asked for it' are raped, and even the police may be thoroughly unsympathetic, although this position is gradually changing.

There is a myth that rape only occurs in dark alleys and with total strangers, but over 50 per cent of the women who contact Rape Crisis Centre in London have had previous contact with the man concerned and over 30 per cent have been raped in their own homes.

To avoid potential sexual assault or rape situations, keep to well-lit streets, walk with purpose and be alert to potentially dangerous situations.

If you think you are being followed, either go into a pub and use the phone to contact a friend, or tell the landlord/lady. If there is nowhere to go, knock at the door of a house and hope that whoever answers will be sensible and sympathetic. If all else fails, run.

Sometimes it is possible to talk an aggressor out of a situation, by using your wits to engage him in conversation until you can make a run for it or you can get a passer-by or neighbour to offer assistance.

There are still myths that all women secretly want to be raped and that only bad women are victims. The truth is that rape is not sexual intercourse in the wrong place and at the wrong time, but an act of violence. Women of all ages, races and lifestyles are potential victims. A man who rapes is not a sex-starved maniac, either: 63 per cent of the cases dealt with by the Rape Crisis Centre in its first six months were planned.

To avoid trouble as far as possible, take time to get to know any new acquaintances. Wait until you are fairly sure of your ground before you get into situations which could lead to problems. Do not invite men home to your flat if you are on your own, or when you have only just met them.

If you are raped or sexually assaulted, try to contact a close woman friend. If you decide to report the case to the police you should do so at once, certainly before you wash or change your clothes.

Reporting rape is not a pleasant experience and some police are less than helpful or downright antagonistic. You may be interviewed by a male police officer but you can insist on being interviewed by a policewoman if you wish.

Whatever you decide to do about reporting rape it is essential you see a doctor as soon as possible to check for VD, pregnancy or injury. This is vital.

In London, the Rape Crisis Centre has a 24-hour telephone line for women and girls who have been raped or sexually assaulted. If you want to talk to another woman or need legal or medical information you can ring at any time; emergency or not, the service is free and confidential.

Outside London there is a network of centres, mainly in large cities.

INCEST

'Incest' means sexual relations between close relatives such as brother and sister, father and daughter or mother and son. A sexual relationship between half-brothers and sisters is also incestuous. (A sexual relationship between cousins is not.) Although the subject is considered taboo in many circles, it is more common that was previously realized.

If you are being bothered in this way you do not have to put up with it, but bringing the matter out into the open could have distressing consequences for the rest of the family. Threatening to go to the police may stop the problem, or you could contact the Albany Trust, which provides counselling on all sexual matters in strict confidence, or ring the Samaritans.

Moving out of your home is probably the least destructive way to deal with the matter, but in any case you will almost certainly need counselling to heal the emotional damage.

CHAPTER 10

Making the most of yourself

It is important to feel good about yourself, and that involves making the best of your looks – highlighting good points and minimizing bad ones. Read the fashion magazines that tell you what is in style but take care not to dress for fashion's sake rather than finding what suits you. A healthy vitality is always attractive yet non-threatening: read how to acquire it in Chapter 7. Dressing with flair makes good sense. Many potentially successful women miss out on this one vital aspect of their professionalism. Dressing well is more important in some cases than others, especially in fields such as advertising or journalism; people's first impressions of your clothes and general style are important and tend to last. Do not assume that because you are desk-bound or not on view to the public what you wear does not matter. Good dress sense and style are still potent weapons.

Aim for a look that is feminine without being overtly sexy. Leave skirts split to the thigh or blouses that plunge to the waist for your social life. They have no place at work – unless you work in a night-club. The same applies to very heavy make-up or long, dangling jewellery. You may look devastatingly attractive but you will not be taken seriously. Keep sexy dressing for your private life.

There used to be a 'uniform' that the young executive woman was supposed to wear. It often consisted of a neat, tailored suit, severe blouse, court shoes and a non-frivolous hairstyle. The idea was that she would blend into the background with men aiming at the top and compete with them at their own game.

That rather boring style of dressing has largely gone now, though in certain fields such as law or banking the style of dress is still rather conservative.

For the most part, there is now far more flexibility in choosing what to wear and the name of the game is to be appropriately dressed without being a clone of every other woman executive within the management hierarchy.

Do not worry about not having many clothes. Invest in the best skirt and jacket or matching blouse and skirt that you can afford, then ring the changes with carefully chosen wardrobe fillers such as sweaters, waistcoats or sleeveless jackets, or softly-fitting jackets that can also double up as blouses. One jacket with two skirts, one slimline and one in an A-line or flaired style, for example, will serve you well as you will get more wear out of the skirts than the jacket.

Dark colours with small patterns or plain textures work well, and so do stripes, depending on your own size and shape. Leave large, splashy prints and pastel 'baby' colours alone. Avoid clothes that fit too tightly or cling, as well as over-short skirts and fussy details.

Take care to see that your clothes look good when you buy them. Natural fibres such as wool and cotton usually keep their appearance better than man-made fabrics. Check that shoulders fit and hems are even: nothing reveals lack of quality more than a wavy hemline. Do not wear anything that pulls across the bust or bottom or in any way draws attention to your figure except to emphasize that you are neat and trim.

Invest in one stylish dress that you can wear to any special function you may have to attend. People often laugh at the concept of the 'little black dress', but whether it is black or red or purple it really means a basic dress than can always be played up or dressed down depending on the occasion.

Jewellery needs to be carefully chosen too. Avoid fussy necklaces or bracelets in the office, and do not go in for long, dangling ear-rings. Avoid pendants with your name on them. Carefully chosen accessories can say a lot about you. You do not need to wear precious stones or gold, but if you buy costume or 'fun' jewellery make sure that it is not too way out, and if it is frankly fake, make sure it looks a good fake.

Buy quality accessories. Leather shoes are more comfortable to wear and look good. It is important to choose shoes for comfort as well as style. The last thing you need on a busy, stressful day is to find that your feet are killing you.

Have two or three good pairs in basic colours and ring the changes so that you do not have to wear the same pair every day. Have the heels and soles repaired as soon as they need it, and put the shoes away on shoe-trees to help them keep their shape.

Make sure the handbag you use is big enough for everything you need to put in it. It is better to go around with a large bag rather than a small one that is full to bursting and thoroughly out of shape.

A briefcase, if you use one, needs to be of quality too. If you cannot afford a really good one, use a canvas tote-bag or a fashionable bag that suits your style of dressing and can just be discarded when it shows signs of wear.

HAIRSTYLES

The best hairstyle is the one that flatters you and is easy to manage. Choose a style that you can forget about during the day. The cut should be good enough to withstand a strong wind or a shower of rain without the style being completely destroyed.

Shining hair in tip-top condition shows that you care about yourself and pay attention to such matters as grooming. Have your hair cut as often as you need – every six weeks to two months for most people – and make sure the cut is the best one you can find in your town. Long hair is not to be recommended for a budding executive. Keep your hair above shoulder length unless you wear it up.

Do not be afraid of giving your hair a colour lift if it needs it. Who needs mousey hair? If you have the odd grey hair (yes, even teenagers can find them) invest in a good colour rinse or blond streaks.

MAKE-UP

Whether you wear make-up or not, you will need to cultivate a good, clear, healthy skin, free of blemishes. Eat well (see Chapter 7) and keep skin scrupulously clean. Treat any blemishes or spots with a medicated stick and use a medicated facial wash at night. Use plenty of moisturizer.

Discreet make-up will emphasize your executive image. See your eyebrows are brushed into a neat arch. Keep way-out colours, over-strong eye make-up or cheek colours for another time and place. Make up in a good light so that you never end up with too much colour or harsh edges. Nothing looks worse than a streaky colour tone with unevenly blended edges around the ears and jawline.

If you wear foundation, check carefully to see that it is the right colour for you. Do not forget that your skin will change colour through the year, especially during the summer. Apply foundation sparingly with a damp, cosmetic sponge rather than with your fingers.

Check that your make-up still looks good in the office light. Fluorescent bulbs can be very cruel and can distort colours too.

Make sure you do not leave lipstick marks all over the office crockery.

Be prepared for a discreet re-touch to your make-up during the day. Keep a mini survival kit in an office drawer including tissues, a hand mirror and a nail file for any necessary repairs. A good clothes brush is a must, too.

Hands are constantly on show in an office, so keep your nails well manicured; if you use nail varnish, see that it is always well applied and never leave it on if it becomes chipped. But heed the warning of one high-powered woman executive who maintained she could always tell a girl who did not have enough work to do if she had immaculately varnished nails.

DISGUISING FIGURE FAULTS
Unfortunately very few of us have perfect figures, even if there were one standard for perfection – which there is not. What you do need however, is to present an over-all attractive appearance.

Lack of height can work against you in an executive role, though some of it may be within your own power to change. Do you unconsciously or even consciously feel that small is appealing, and do you play the helpless little woman? If you do, it is up to you to change it. Most people believe that height equals authority. Looking down on someone is a psychological bonus. Although you cannot do much about your height it is possible to minimize many adverse effects. You can create an illusion of extra inches by keeping to matching or toning tops and bottoms to outfits, so that there is an unbroken line. Tone tights and shoes into the same colour role and you will have gained extra inches. Keep most of your accessory interest near your face. Do not wear contrasting belts that cut you in two. Make use of vertical stripes and avoid any details such as frills or patterned borders that will attract attention downwards to your hemline.

If you are overweight you do not need me to tell you that this will work against your professional image, or that the only answer is to diet and exercise until you have scaled down. Nevertheless, while this is happening remember that most of the tips for looking taller apply to looking slimmer too. Keep to dark colours and do not wear clingy fabrics. See your clothes fit you and stop wearing garments that are obviously too tight. Dark colours will help to play down parts of your figure you do not want noticed. Loose, easy styles are a god-send if you need to scale down, but do not overdo the baggy look or you may end up looking like orphan Annie.

GROOMING
Good grooming says a lot about you as a person. It shows that you pay attention to detail and your fastidiousness will spill

over into your attitude to work. Grooming is an important part of the total image you are putting together. People who are going places do not have broken-down heels on their shoes, dragging hemlines, frayed cuffs or buttons missing from jackets.

Pay attention not only to personal grooming but also see that your clothes are dry-cleaned or laundered as soon as necessary and minor repairs coped with as soon as is necessary.

Keep a good-quality clothes brush in your office drawer and make a point of brushing your jacket or skirt regularly. If you are really stuck with dog or cat hairs, remove them with sticky tape. Wipe over collars and cuffs with a dry-cleaning solvent as you take off your jacket or sweater. It will remove most of a make-up mark or the odd stain. Watch out for grease spots or coffee stains and deal with them immediately if possible.

Washable clothes are more practical than those that need to be dry-cleaned every time, but do follow the fabric care instructions on the label (see pages 32–3). Dry-clean clothes as often as they need it, and if you find a persistent stain tell the assistant what you think it is as you hand it over the counter.

ARE YOU IN GOOD VOICE?

Good, clear diction and a pleasant manner are essential tools of the trade in communicating with people at all levels. If you are unhappy about the way you speak, consider taking a public speaking course at evening classes. These are not only for would-be politicians or budding actresses but will help you develop effective speech for every occasion. By learning to think on your feet at public-speaking classes you will develop valuable communication skills for all occasions – business meetings, telephone calls, talking to customers and coping with formal social functions.

Do not try to eliminate a regional accent. You should be proud of it, and fortunately the idea that the only acceptable 'professional' voice is that of a BBC announcer died the death long ago.

Quality of voice is important too. Does it give you a shock when you hear your voice played back on a tape-recorder? Do people ever mimic the way you speak, or constantly interrupt you when you are making a point? Discourteous though it may be, there may be something in it for you to learn.

Your voice may not have a pleasant tone. It could be squeaky or strident. You may use unfortunate expressions or mispronounce words without even realizing what you are doing.

If you have any doubts, listen to yourself on a tape-recorder.

Leave it on while you are talking to a friend or reading a page from a book or report. Afterwards play it back and see how it sounds. It is more than likely that you will hate what you hear.

Many women speak at too high a pitch. If you are one of them, make a conscious effort to pitch your voice lower. Women also have a tendency to giggle or whine – both unattractive traits socially, but disastrous in business life. It takes effort to undo such habits, but it can and must be done.

You may also have nagging fears that you are sometimes ungrammatical or that you mispronounce words. Listen to the way actors, actresses and announcers speak on radio and TV. Most are grammatical and listening carefully may help you to pinpoint one or two failings of your own. If you are not sure how to pronounce a word, look it up in the dictionary. Read the preface in the front that gives you the pronunciation key so that you can work out the pronunciation of the word in question.

Sometimes for reasons beyond our control we may use unacceptable expressions in everyday speech. If swearing, for example, has become a habit you have dropped into, you may have to make a determined effort to eliminate it. However trendy the circles in which we move there are still many people who object to such behaviour. Swearing *never* makes a good impression.

If you find people using words you do not understand, get back to the dictionary again to find out what they mean. Enlarge your vocabulary by playing Scrabble or doing crosswords. Reading helps enormously, too – any books, both fiction and non-fiction; books will also give you the raw material for becoming a better all-round conversationalist.

CHAPTER 11

A chance to learn

Learning is a continuing process, not something that stops dead when you leave school or college.

Fortunately we can learn about things and people for the rest of our lives. It is just part of the fun and exhilaration of maturing. You can learn a great deal from taking part in community projects (Chapter 12) or from taking up a hobby and becoming an expert in a subject that interests you.

You may want to learn at a very easy pace, at evening classes, where you can often begin to learn the rudiments of a subject that will help you get on in your job, such as book-keeping or typing, or the basics of a language; or you could master the technicalities of a spare-time occupation that will earn you money.

Evening classes are available to everyone, and if you live in or near a large town or city you will have a wide variety to choose from. Even after the cutbacks of the past few years they are still very cheap, and if you are unemployed you will probably be entitled to a considerable reduction in fees.

If you want to take your learning a step further you can attend summer schools or take part in one of the many activity holidays organized all over Britain. Here you can speed up learning about your hobby during a week's holiday, probably in an old country house or at a college that is empty for the summer break; you will be given expert tuition, meet like-minded people and have a congenial holiday at the same time. Costs vary widely; some holidays are subsidized by the local councils, though only for people living in that area.

A lot of these holidays focus on sports, but by no means all of them. You might be able to learn about antiques, which could stand you in good stead if you have ever had a pipe-dream about running an antiques business. You can study vegetarian cooking, creative writing or photography. The English Tourist Board publish a booklet, *Activity and Hobby Holidays*, which might give you some ideas; otherwise, look at the classified advertisements in national newspapers.

YOUTH TRAINING SCHEME

If you are 16 or 17 and have just left school ask your local Careers Office about the Youth Training Scheme. It has been set up to offer training and work experience, and at the end you will be given a certificate to show what you have done.

If you already have a job, the Youth Training Scheme can help. You will be trained how to do the job and also find out about other jobs within your firm and outside. By enrolling for the Youth Training Scheme as an employee you will be paid the normal rate for the job. If you join the scheme when you are unemployed you will be given a weekly allowance instead. You may work in a local firm or on a special scheme or a community project. You will not have to pay National Insurance or income tax and will be given paid holidays. You will not necessarily be offered a permanent job after your year is up, but it will have given you a real insight into what work, as opposed to school, is really like.

TOPS SCHEME

If you are at least 19 years old and have been away from full-time education for at least two years you could enrol for a Training Opportunities Scheme. (Different criteria operate if you are disabled.) The courses are designed to help people train for a job and one of the conditions of being accepted is that you intend to use the skill you acquire for future employment. There is a wide choice of training, though it varies from one part of the country to another. The course can last for anything between one and 12 months; you are paid an allowance while you are on the course, and something towards the cost of travel. You may have to wait a while to go on the course you choose, and you will have to take an aptitude test first. For advice and further information ask at your local Jobcentre.

LOCAL SCHEMES

In many towns there are various schemes open to unemployed school-leavers. You may find there is a workshop where you can go to train for a better job. Very often these schemes help to develop practical skills such as mending bikes, decorating, making jewellery or machine knitting. Enquire at your local council offices or ask your careers officer.

PART-TIME STUDY WHILE UNEMPLOYED

If you are unemployed you may be able to take a part-time college course for up to 21 hours a week without affecting your eligibility for supplementary benefit. You have to keep looking for a job and be prepared to leave the course if you find one. Ask for details at your careers office.

The National Institute of Adult Continuing Education deals with general enquiries about adult education. If the enquiry is outside its scope the institute will try to pass it on to the appropriate quarter.

An 'Educational Guidance Services for Adults' list is printed in the annual *Year Book of Adult Continuing Education* which you should be able to see in your local library. The organizations listed, under regions, give advice on educational opportunities available locally.

If you want to find out more about training, further education and jobs in your area ask your careers officer or contact the Regional Advisory Council for Further Education in your area (part of the DES).

The Department of Education and Science publishes the booklet *Choosing at 16*, of which your careers officer should have a copy. It also publishes a booklet entitled *What Next After School?* You should be able to get one from your careers officer.

The Certificate of Pre-vocational Education (CPVE), also known as the 17-plus, is for 16-year-olds who would like to spend a further year in full-time education but on a practical rather than an academic course.

The CPVE certificate is awarded after students have completed one of the following courses: Foundation Course and Vocational Preparation (General) course of the City and Guilds; the General Awards of the Business and Technician Education Council (BTEC), in the business field; the Royal Society of Arts (RSA) Vocational Preparation Clerical and Distribution course and Basic Clerical Procedures course. Ask your careers officer for more information.

The Careers and Occupational Information Centre publishes books and leaflets (ask your careers teacher or try your local library). *Ways to Work* is aimed at people beginning to think about a job.

CITY AND GUILDS

The City and Guilds of London Institute provides courses and examinations for technical and craft vocations. The certificates are evidence of various levels of competence and are highly regarded in industry.

Courses are held in technical colleges of further education and schools, and are either part-time or full-time; they are often run on a day-release basis. The subjects cover a wide range, including home economics and creative studies, travel and tourism, hotel management and catering, and computer subjects, to name just a few. For more information ask at any technical college, or at the Careers Advisory Service office of your local education authority.

NATIONAL EXTENSION COLLEGE
The NEC offers home study courses which include O- and A-level GCE. There are 70 courses to choose from and guidance is given on the choice of course before enrolment.

Some home students are given grants by their local education authority, so it is worth enquiring whether you might be eligible for one.

Also offered are business and professional courses such as 'Communications in Business', practical business law, computing and preparatory courses for Open University.

OPEN UNIVERSITY
Courses are designed for home study, by post, in conjunction with television and radio programmes, and may include attending a summer school for one week in the year. Some courses are academic and can lead to a BA degree. They are awarded on a system of credits – a minimum of six for a BA. Each student has a course tutor and can attend local centres for study. Write to the Open University for the booklet *Guide for Applicants for BA Degree Courses*.

The Associate Student Programme offers study courses in, for example, the new technologies, professional and scientific updating and a number of community education courses; these are listed in the booklet *Guide to the Associate Student Programme*, also available from the Open University.

The Open University has special arrangements for disabled students (see Chapter 13).

UNIVERSITY ENTRANCE
The Universities' Central Council on Admissions (UCCA) processes all students' applications for admission to full-time first degree courses at universities in the UK. Write for an explanatory leaflet if your school does not provide copies.

GRANTS FOR STUDENTS
If you have been given a place on a 'designated' course and satisfy qualifying conditions you will be eligible for a grant. The amount will depend on your parents' income, as it assumed that they will contribute towards your upkeep. This will still be the

case if you marry while studying: your parents will be expected to continue contributing to your maintenance.

A discretionary grant is given by local education authorities; each decides its own policy so conditions vary according to area. Write to your local education authority for information. A brief guide entitled *Grants to Students* is available from the Department of Education and Science.

For alternative sources of grants consult the *Director of Grant-making Trusts* published by the Charities Aid Foundation, which should be available at your local library. The Educational Grants Advisory Service of the Family Welfare Association may be able to advise on alternative sources of funds.

DEEDS OF COVENANT
If you are a student your parents can make you payments under a deed of covenant and thereby save tax. Ask at your local Inland Revenue offices for their form IR47.

CHAPTER 12

Time to spare

We all have time to spare in varying degrees, though for some unemployment may mean we have too much, while for others spare time may be an odd evening at home or a weekend afternoon when plans have fallen through. Some of the suggestions in this section for ways to use your leisure time have been discussed in Chapter 8, but if you have time to spare on a longer-term basis there are many ways of filling it.

You may decide to make a break between leaving school and going to university or out to work. This is a sensible idea, for several reasons. It gives you a chance to see the real world outside the narrow confines of an educational environment, and a rest from study before you knuckle down once again to work for qualifications. Once you have started a job your ambitions and career path may make it impossible for you ever again to take time off for a different type of experience. Marriage and parenthood may also prevent your breaking away to do something totally different. On the other hand, you may find it possible to go to work for a year after school and then take off, having acquired some work experience and perhaps some savings to fall back on.

Sometimes you can learn a foreign language and earn pocket money as well by working as an *au pair* abroad. Usually girls find jobs through an established agency and work for anything between six months and a year in a family, looking after children and doing light domestic chores. With a pleasant family, willing to make you feel at home and give you the opportunity to go out and meet friends, it can be a wonderful way to see another country. *The Lady* magazine, published weekly, contains classified advertisements placed by families requiring *au pairs* and mothers' helps both in Britain and abroad. It also has many advertisements from *au pair* agencies.

Find out as much as you can about the family before you accept the job and tell them about yourself in the letters you exchange. It is difficult to get to know anyone through an exchange of letters so get as many details as you can. Try to find out some of the customs and conditions you may meet in the country. Conditions in Middle Eastern countries, for example, may be very different from anything you have encountered in Britain, so take particular care if you are planning to stay with a family from a different cultural background. Find out the laws relating to your personal freedom before you take the job.

VOLUNTARY WORK

If you are able to work for basic expenses only, there are many exciting schemes open to you.

Community Service Volunteers (CSV) is a national volunteer agency that matches volunteers all over Britain with community service projects. Anyone from 16 to 35 is eligible and no one is rejected. Severely disabled people have been able to take part in the scheme and have thus discovered a wonderful way to feel wanted and useful within the community.

The duties are varied but may include working with the physically and mentally handicapped, the elderly, the homeless or young offenders. Placements are usually for between four months and a year. All volunteers receive travelling and other out-of-pocket expenses within the UK, full board and lodging and pocket money. Write to CSV for more details and an application form.

Voluntary Service Overseas (VSO) now looks for qualified people to help in its overseas programmes in the Third World. Its greatest need is for those qualified in agriculture, health, education or with technical qualifications. Candidates must be between 20 and 65 and have no dependants. You need special qualities of character to undertake the rigours of working for a minimum of two years in often isolated and primitive areas (at least by Western standards). You need to be self-reliant, adaptable, resilient and sensitive to be able to respond to people's needs. All volunteers stress that they learn more from the experience than they pass on.

Candidates accepted for overseas work have their return air fare paid plus equipment and re-equipment grants. A mid-tour grant is also paid after one year. VSO will also play Class III National Insurance or Class I where appropriate. You are also covered by medical insurance whilst overseas. Accommodation is provided and pay is on a basis comparable to that of a local worker.

You can also help in other ways in the UK by joining local groups and assisting with fund-raising and publicity. VSO is a non-governmental organization.

For more information write to VSO enclosing a large s.a.e.

World Community Development Service (WCDS) runs a

Junior Volunteers Scheme for young people aged 18 upwards. They are sent for a period of six months or one year to live and work in development projects in India, Sri Lanka and Kenya. The volunteers are attached to indigenous organizations and may work in children's centres, with medical and agricultural staff, or in schools teaching practical and academic subjects such as English.

The aim of the scheme is mainly educational. The volunteers benefit personally by learning about a different society and the meaning of poverty at first hand. WCDS tries to build personal links between Third World communities and those here in Britain. It aims to select young people with an interest in and commitment to development issues who are prepared to play an active part in development education on their return. Returned volunteers are responsible for the running of WCDS itself and assist in the selection and orientation of new volunteers.

Volunteers begin their periods abroad in September and February. Selection takes place by an initial interview and a selection weekend. The cost to the volunteer is £780 for a six-month placement and £830 for one year. WCDS provides a seven-day orientation course, return air fare, health insurance and a monthly stipend appropriate to the placement. For further details, write to WCDS enclosing an s.a.e.

Project Trust sends young people overseas between school and university or beginning a career. Only school-leavers between 17 and 19 are accepted. Projects last between 10 and 12 months and are all outside Europe, mainly in Africa, Australia, the Caribbean and the Far and Middle East. Applications, accompanied by a large s.a.e., should be in by 1 January for departure overseas by September.

The Central Bureau for Educational Visits and Exchanges produces *Volunteer Work Abroad*, listing 40 organizations which send volunteers abroad and information about each project, age limits, qualifications required, etc. (£2.50 inc. p. & p.). It also produces *Working Holidays*, which provides details of opportunities in several countries including the USA (£3.60 inc. p. & p.).

International Voluntary Service provides for people of all races, creeds and politics to unite in giving useful service to the community. There are three main ways to volunteer. First, you can join an international work camp, for between two and four weeks. These are held in the UK and in Eastern and Western Europe, and there are also exchanges, often of longer duration, with Africa, Asia and North America. Volunteers must be over 18. Work may include helping in psychiatric hospitals, assisting

119

with holidays for handicapped children, running children's play schemes and working with minority groups.

Secondly, there is long-term service in the Third World. Volunteers serve for two or more years and live with the community in which they work. They contribute practical skills that are lacking locally and train local people to take over when they leave. Service is mainly in Botswana, Lesotho, Mozambique, Swaziland and occasionally other African and Asian countries.

A third form of service is with local groups within the UK. There is a network of about 30 groups which work within local communities, and volunteers help with their projects.

Volunteers must become members of IVS, pay a small registration fee and meet their own travel expenses. Food and basic accommodation are provided free. For more details, write to IVS enclosing an s.a.e.

Gap Activity Projects Ltd. offers employment abroad to school-leavers waiting to go to university. They must be 18 either before or whilst abroad. Send an s.a.e. for information.

Time Between is a guide to opportunities for work and service before, during and after higher education. Write for a copy, enclosing an s.a.e., to the Careers Research and Advisory Centre.

A Place for You Overseas? is a series of information sheets available to school-leavers and students, and also qualified people, from Christians Abroad; topics include volunteer work, work camps and opportunities for school-leavers. Send an s.a.e. for leaflets and general advice.

There are hundred of societies that could do with your help. The choice of projects and types of work available is enormous. Your local social services department may be able to put you in touch with some of them, or look in *Yellow Pages* under Charitable and Benevolent Organizations or Social Services and Welfare Organizations. You may find your town has a volunteer bureau for the recruitment of volunteer workers which could put you in touch with work you would enjoy. Failing that, ask your local Citizens' Advice Bureau for suggestions.

Individual organizations are listed in the handbook *Voluntary Organisations: an NCVO Directory* (£5.90 inc. p. & p. from Macdonald & Evans), which lists over 700 national organizations with information about the activities and objectives of each.

The Volunteer Centre is the national advisory agency on voluntary work, providing information, advice and training service to all volunteer bureaux. If you cannot find the address of your local volunteer bureau in the telephone directory, try your local Citizens' Advice Bureau or Town Hall information desk, or contact the Volunteer Centre.

Addresses of councils for voluntary service, rural community councils and community associations can be obtained from the National Council for Voluntary Organizations (send an s.a.e.).

The National Youth Bureau produces a *Guide to Voluntary Work Opportunities* available from the Young Volunteers Resources Unit (send an A4 s.a.e. with a 33p stamp).

If you feel strongly about conservation, you might enjoy working with like-minded people on projects all over Britain. The projects tackled by Conservation Volunteers vary from improving footpaths, dredging lakes and re-building sluices to building dry-stone walls. Camps provide accommodation, usually indoors in village halls and schools or volunteer centres. To attend, you must be over 16 and become a member of Conservation Volunteers (subscription £5.00); volunteers normally pay their own fares and contribute from £1.35 to £2.00 a day (depending on the season) towards food and accommodation. Work is usually over a week or two and consists of an 8-hour day with one free day a week. It is strenuous but fun, and a wonderful way to have an unusual holiday.

Write for details of forthcoming projects to the British Trust for Conservation Volunteers.

The Winged Fellowship Trust arranges holidays for handicapped people at various centres and is pleased to hear from responsible, able-bodied volunteers who can lend a hand and enter into a community spirit. You may find yourself taking a wheelchair patient for a walk, buttering the bread for tea or helping a handicapped person to wash. Whilst most volunteers are required for one or two weeks during the summer, they are sometimes needed at other times of the year. You pay your own fare but receive full board and lodging free. Write to the Trust for more information.

Pensioners' Link (formerly known as Task Force) works with pensioners in London. Volunteers aim to work in partnership with pensioners to provide resources and information, and the sort of support that enables them to do things for themselves. Helpers also arrange services which are outside the scope of the social services: you may be called upon to help establish a pensioners' club, book speakers, raise funds or organize meetings, for example. They also provide assistance for housebound pensioners by offering them regular visits and help with shopping expeditions. Write for details to Pensioners' Link enclosing an s.a.e.

WORKING HOLIDAYS
You can get an idea of the sort of work available from Vacation Work, which publishes a directory of summer jobs in Britain (£3.95). The *Summer Employment Directory of the United States* provides details of summer vacancies of various kinds in the USA (£5.95).

DUKE OF EDINBURGH AWARD SCHEME
This is a programme of activities for people between the ages of 14 and 25, resulting in a bronze, silver or gold award. The scheme is not competitive, and progress is measured in terms of individual effort and improvement.

Each award covers the fields of community service, an expedition, a skill such as a hobby, topic of study or some other leisure interest which could be from starting an aquarium to stamp-collecting, and physical recreation, for which you take up a physical activity for at least six weeks and reach a given standard or show improvement.

Everyone is qualified to enter and many disabled people have gained awards.

The scheme is frequently run by volunteers, through schools, youth clubs, voluntary organizations and some commercial industry offices.

For details write to the Duke of Edinburgh Award offices.

ROYAL JUBILEE TRUSTS
Three trust funds under the umbrella of the Royal Jubilee Trusts exist to help young volunteers carry out practical projects that will benefit the community and people in need. The grants made are small, but are available to both individuals and groups of volunteers.

The idea for the project should be something not already provided by any other organization, and you need to work out how the project would fund itself once the grant had been exhausted.

The regional committee will look for good ideas and commitment before making grants; the projects themselves can range from building canoes adapted to the needs of the disabled to starting a children's radio station in a local hospital or organizing an inshore rescue service. (These are just a sample of recent projects that have been funded since Jubilee Year.)

If you have an idea or want to know more about the scheme, write for guidelines and an application form to the Director of the Royal Jubilee Trusts at the appropriate regional address.

CHAPTER 13

If you are disabled

If you are disabled you have probably worked hard to lead as near normal a life as possible. You have discovered how to overcome some difficulties and learned to live with others and to live, with the support of your family and friends, a happy life.

In many cases, when it is time to leave home your needs will be very much the same as those of other young people in that you will be simultaneously excited and apprehensive about the practicalities of how you will cope. In many instances you will cope as well as any other person, but you may be able to call upon a little extra support or make a few special arrangements that will make all the difference to settling down away from home.

You will probably already be in touch with special societies that deal with your particular disability. Many of them have helpful leaflets or residential training schools to help you bridge the gap between full-time education and work.

Some will offer training for work in their own specialized workshops, others will provide training to enable you to take a job in the outside world.

ATTENDING COLLEGE

The National Bureau for Handicapped Students receives many enquiries from students and colleges alike. Colleges now seem much more aware of their responsibilities towards handicapped students; however, not all colleges seem able to put them into practice.

If you are likely to qualify academically for entry to college, you should apply for an interview.

If you are at school your careers teacher or careers officer should be able to help you. The Bureau publishes an information sheet, *Applying to Higher Education*, which is also available on tape.

Many colleges suggest that if you are worried about their facilities you should write to their Adviser for Handicapped Students (most colleges now have a member of staff with this responsibility).

You may be invited to make an informal visit, but in any case the reply you receive will indicate the attitude of the college and if it appears negative you may be better off concentrating on those that appear more helpful.

You may feel you must play down your disability at a formal interview, but once you have been offered a place it is a good idea to ask if you can go back again to have another look and discuss any special needs.

Most handicapped students are offered accommodation in a hall of residence or hostel where one is available. It is important to see the type of accommodation you will be offered to assess whether it is suitable and whether it can accommodate any special equipment you will need: wheelchair access, suitable lavatories or, for the blind, strong shelving for large, heavy Braille books.

You may encounter self-catering arrangements, and although these will probably not be a problem it is a good idea to get used to moving around the kitchen in your own home and doing normal domestic chores.

SETTLING IN

All new students experience some trepidation on leaving home or settling into a new way of life, and you will be no exception. You may find the college is rather large compared with the school you have been used to. You may have to walk a long way to various classes and it may take you longer than some of the other students.

It may be possible for you to arrive a day or two early, ahead of anyone else, to get the lie of the land; you would also have time to talk to some of the staff. It would be sensible to sit down with someone and discuss your disability frankly: this person could become your link with the rest of the staff and could alert them to any special problems, such as whether you need to be in a good light or whether you should sit near the front of the class.

Any special equipment necessary to enable you to study is usually provided by the college. Where it is not available, or if you are working at home, you could apply to your local education authority. Some aids are available locally through the DHSS, so make your enquiries there. Otherwise, certain voluntary organizations may be able to help.

Sometimes it is possible to have your travelling costs subsidized, so if you need assistance ask your local education authority. (Your claim will probably have to be supported by a social worker.)

DISABLED STUDENT'S ALLOWANCE
Students on grants are able to claim an additional allowance if they can show that extra expenditure is necessary as a result of their disability. Claims should be made to the local education authority.

The Snowdon Award Scheme provides grants for physically handicapped people between 17 and 25 to help them undertake further education or training. Candidates must provide evidence that their financial circumstances, coupled with the problems of disability, are an obstacle to their taking advantage of such an opportunity. Each bursary is for up to £1,000 per annum for a maximum of two years.

Application forms can be obtained from Action Research for the Crippled Child.

FINDING WORK
Your careers teacher, officer or adviser will have discussed with you your own work prospects. The support society for your own disability will also be able to give you guidance and may offer special training.

As soon as you leave school or college you should register under the Disabled Persons (Employment) Act. A Disablement Resettlement Officer (DRO) attached to your Jobcentre will see you and, if necessary, arrange for you to be certified as disabled. The main conditions of registration are that your disability is likely to last for more than twelve months, that you are substantially handicapped in finding and keeping employment and that you really want a job and are likely to be able to keep it if you find one.

The Disablement Resettlement Officer's aim is to help you reach your true potential and where appropriate will give advice on initial assessment of your capabilities, suggest further appropriate training, residential or otherwise.

The DRO is also responsible for seeing that local firms operate the full quota scheme that requires those with 20 or more employees to employ 3 per cent disabled people.

YOUTH TRAINING SCHEME
The Youth Training Scheme (see Chapter 11) has special rules concerning the eligibility of disabled young people, who are able to take part in the scheme up to the age of 21.

The Careers Service is available to all handicapped people, and indeed all young people attending full- or part-time education; you may find that there is a specialist careers officer for handicapped people in your area.

You may be asked to attend an assessment centre, where an expert will assess your skills and make recommendations about your future: for example, whether you should register for further training, take sheltered employment or seek work through the DRO.

It may be recommended that you should take a TOPS course. These courses offer free training, with allowances as well as free midday meals and lodging allowances where appropriate. The rules outlined on page 113 are relaxed for disabled students. Ask for details of the TOPS schemes at your local Jobcentre.

The Training Service Agency arranges residential courses for suitable disabled people referred to them through the Careers Service or DRO. A leaflet, *Residential Training for Disabled People* (TSA L65), is obtainable from Jobcentres and DROs. Training and accommodation are free and tax-free allowances are also paid to help with travel. For details of allowances ask for leaflet TSA L9.

OPEN UNIVERSITY

The Open University has special facilities for disabled students; it may discriminate in favour of them and allow them to queue-jump in order to gain admission. Eligibility depends on certain conditions laid down by the Admissions Committee. However, the same academic standards are required for disabled students as for any other, though there are special procedures for examination and assessment.

A regular newsletter is sent three times a year to disabled students, and visually handicapped or hearing-impaired students can attend a weekend residential induction course before starting their studies.

Special learning materials such as cassettes or transcripts are also available.

MENTAL HANDICAP

Various avenues are open to anyone with a mental handicap, in terms of both higher education and of jobs. Some colleges and technical colleges offer special courses specifically run for handicapped people. Ask your local education authority what is available in your area.

A fact sheet is available that lists voluntary establishments where further education, vocational training and assessment, and also sheltered employment for school-leavers, are provided. It is available from the Voluntary Council for Handicapped Children, c/o National Children's Bureau. Pathway Employment Service is a work preparation and job scheme run by MenCap. Employment officers take referrals of mentally handicapped people who may be suitable for outside employment. Ask the DRO, contacted via the local Jobcentre, or your social worker or headteacher at school.

After their potential has been assessed, candidates have an initial training programme and are then placed with a firm for a probationary period. Write to MenCap for more details.

The UK Sports Association for People with Mental Handicap, which operates regionally, co-ordinates organizations promoting physical activities undertaken by mentally handicapped people. More information is available from the Sports Council.

There are over 500 Gateway clubs which integrate leisure activities for mentally handicapped people and able-bodied helpers. For more information contact the National Federation of Gateway Clubs at MenCap.

LEISURE

There are a vast number of associations that enable handicapped people to engage in sports and hobbies. Whatever your particular interest, there will be some provision for you to take it up.

Make enquiries about what is available locally. You may find that the local swimming bath for instance, has special facilities, or that special times are set aside for organized groups.

Many voluntary organizations provide recreational facilities, and some sports centres have both special facilities and a programme of events.

The British Sports Association for the Disabled will be able to tell you if there is a local association for you to contact.

The Disabled Living Foundation, as well as offering an information service and permanent display of aids, which can be seen and tried out by appointment, has further advisory services on clothing, incontinence, visual handicap, skin conditions, physical recreation and music. A wide range of helpful literature on all these subjects and on the resolution of other daily living problems is published by the Foundation. Write for further details.

SEXUALITY

Most disabled people can have a satisfactory sex life. Obviously there can be difficulties, but most can be overcome. Able-bodied people have problems, too, for which they need to obtain outside help.

The Association for the Sexual and Personal Relationships of the Disabled (SPOD) has a series of helpful and practical advisory leaflets, from the basic *Physically Handicapped People and Sex* to *Intercourse Positions* and *Aids to Sex for the Physically Handicapped.* The Association also operates a counselling and advisory service for disabled people and may be able to arrange personal counselling locally. Write to SPOD for leaflets and advice.

The *London Disabled Gays' Guide* gives extensive details of access and welcome in London pubs, clubs and other venues for homosexuals of both sexes. Available from Gemma (send 50p and a stamp).

YOUR RIGHTS
The *Disability Rights Handbook* is published annually and gives valuable information on benefits, etc. Available from RADAR (£2.00, post free).

CHAPTER 14

Being safe in the city

Being constantly alert to danger as you walk the streets is the best guard against being robbed or mugged.

Looking alert and athletic will often make a potential mugger or robber look for another victim. If you look uncertain, nervous or in a daydream, you will be an obvious target.

The most unlikely-looking people commit crimes, not just furtive-looking men. Handsome, well-dressed males steal, and women and children have been known to snatch handbags.

IN THE STREET

Carry your handbag close to your body. In crowds keep it under your arm; do not leave it swinging from your shoulder, and do not leave your purse on top of your shopping bag. Avoid carrying too much money around with you and keep your credit cards and cheque book in different places. If you are getting money from a bank cash till, put it away and re-zip your bag before you move off.

Be alert to possible hazards. Youths sweeping down the pavement and knocking people to one side are a potential danger. Move out of the way before they reach you. Children rushing around on roller skates or skateboards may be planning to take your bag with them as they coast by. Sometimes a motorcyclist or the pillion passenger will make a snatch as they roar towards you, so do not walk too close to the edge of pavements. Walking too near bushes or buildings can also be a mistake: try to steer a middle course.

Watch pedestrians who try to overtake on the inside, especially if the street is not crowded. You can often detect them in shop window reflections, or, if you are in the dark, you can watch how the shadows of people walking behind you fall.

Be on your guard if anyone stops to ask you the time. Most people have their own watch nowadays and this may merely be a ploy that enables them to snatch yours and any other jewellery you might be wearing.

At night, do not walk in dark alleys or across wasteland. Avoid unlit or deserted car parks.

When you are walking home carry your keys in your hand so that you do not have to wait and fumble at the front door. It could be that someone is lurking out of sight to rush at you and gain entry to the house. Have the keys ready so that you can go straight in as soon as you arrive. If you see anything suspicious when you arrive, such as someone hanging around, walk straight past and call at a neighbour's house to ask for help. The same applies if you think you may surprise a burglar. If you arrive home and find the flat has been entered or you think someone may still be there, do not go in. Just walk on and telephone the police, then go to a neighbour's until the police come. Never tackle intruders on your own or encourage anyone else to do so. Your safety is more important than your possessions and you could get hurt.

If you meet a 'flasher' walk on and try not to express any surprise or shock. Do not say anything and do not ridicule the man. Report the incident to the police as soon as you can and be prepared to give a general description of the person. The same applies should you be assaulted. Although your prime objective must be to get away it helps the police to have a general description – beyond the fact, say, that the man was of medium height and slim build with brown hair.

If you see someone being pestered do not just walk on and ignore the situation. Think how you would appreciate some help if it were you. Very often, if the harassment is verbal, just walking closer to the victim will cause the assailant to back off. If you feel the situation is getting out of hand, go for help.

Take advantage of any self-defence classes that are being run in your area. The scope of these varies widely. Some classes are still very much based on judo or karate training, but others are being aimed more at a system of self-defence for ordinary (and probably unfit) people. Find out whether your local educational authority runs classes or look to see if there are any advertised in the local paper. Go along and watch the class to see if it is what you want before you join.

Being basically fit is a help in any case: criminals are more likely to attack the frail and the elderly than people who are obviously fit and able to take care of themselves. Do not attempt to fight back, however angry you feel, or you could end up being seriously injured.

AT HOME

When you first move into a flat it is sensible to change all the locks: some people distribute spare keys like confetti and may not retrieve them all before they move. Changing the locks will make you feel safer, too. Check that doors and windows are secure. If windows can be opened easily get locks fitted or nail them shut.

Do not put your full name on the door. Just an initial and surname will do. Door chains are a good investment. If one has not already been fitted ask the landlord whether you can have one – and use it.

If your name is in the phone book, use your initials only. If you get an obscene phone call, put the phone down immediately. Do not talk to the caller. If the caller persists, inform the police.

Beware the bogus official. Do not assume that because someone wears a uniform or says he is from the water board it is necessarily true. Anyone who has good reason to enter your home will carry an identity card. Study it carefully, as it is not unknown for criminals to carry forged or faked cards. If in doubt, do not let the caller in until you have phoned his office to check.

Always keep the chain on the door when you answer. Even children can be out to steal, so be wary and make sure you are quite convinced in your own mind before you let anyone over the threshold.

Before you go out make sure that all windows and doors are shut. Do not leave obvious notes in the letter-box displaying your absence. Try not to let milk stand on the doorstep longer than you need to. If you are out at night, leave a light on in a room (not just the hallway); some people also leave the radio on to deter intruders.

Do not leave spare keys in obvious places – or in unobvious ones, for that matter. A thief will know them all. Many thieves are opportunists. Some are teenagers on their way home from school. They may decide on the spur of the moment to break into a flat or house that looks deserted or easy to enter.

Keep a note of the serial numbers of any valuables you possess such as radios and cameras and remember where you have put the list of items. You can have goods etched with your initials. Keep jewellery out of sight when it is not being worn. It is always a good idea to have a colour photograph of your most treasured possessions, for without a visual record it is often difficult for the police to track down the owner of recovered stolen goods.

If you have a bicycle keep it locked away, out of sight if possible. Failing that, lock your bicycle to something like railings or a lamp-post when you leave it. Make sure you can give an accurate description of it to the police if it is stolen, and note the serial number. Ask about cycle coding. Under this scheme your postcode and house number are stamped on the bottom bracket so your cycle can be identified no matter where it is found.

IN THE CAR
As far as you can, travel on main or well-used roads. Keep all passenger doors locked while you are in the car and most particularly when you leave it. Always lock the driver's door with the key so you know you have it with you and have not inadvertently locked it inside.

When you return to the car always check it before you get in, especially behind the front seats. Try not to leave your car in a dark place, along a badly lit side road or in an unlit car park.

Do not leave any property visible. Lock it in the boot or put it in the dashboard or under the seats. Do not ever leave valuables in the car.

If you are followed home and you are not likely to find anyone in, do not get out of the car. Lock all the doors, including your driver's door, and put the headlights full on until you can attract help.

PUBLIC TRANSPORT
Avoid isolated bus stops as far as possible. However tempted you may be, do not accept lifts from anyone who offers unless the person is known to you.

Sit downstairs on buses, just inside the door or near the driver. In the underground or train always sit in an open compartment. If you find yourself on your own or with only one other person, move to another compartment.

CHAPTER 15

You, the citizen

Being a fully-fledged adult means you have certain rights and responsibilities. You are expected to keep to the 'rules', but to do so you must know what they are. It is in your own interests to know as much as possible about how the world expects you to behave, and what you in turn can expect of others.

CONSUMER WISDOM

When you first have money of your own, you may feel like going on a long spending spree. But you will have plenty of demands made on your cash, and it is important to become a canny shopper. Look for value for money regardless of the actual price. If the goods are unbelievably cheap, ask yourself why. Perhaps they have 'fallen off the back of a lorry', or they may be so badly made that they will not last, and what looks like something cheap could turn out to be expensive if you have to replace it after a few months.

It is also important to know your rights as a shopper. There are laws to protect you, and it is up to you to know about them.

When you buy something you and the vendor are making a contract and it is the shop or person that sells to you that has to sort out your complaint if you have one later on.

The law, in the shape of the Sale of Goods Act, states that the goods you buy should be of merchantable quality. That means that they must be suitable for the purpose for which they were intended. If a heel falls off your new shoes within a few days of buying them you are entitled to take them back, but if your new fashion boots let in water the shop could claim that you should have known they were not waterproof and you might not have a case. Secondly, the goods must be as described, so keep the packaging or make a note of what was said on the display counter. Thirdly, goods must be fit for any particular purpose that was suggested to you: if the salesperson says the vase you are buying will hold water without leaking, it should do just that, otherwise you have a right to redress.

Take faulty goods back as soon as possible to the shop where you bought them. If the item was given to you as a present, embarrassing though it may be you will have to ask the person who gave it to you to make the claim.

If you are returning goods for any of the three reasons outlined above you do not have to accept a credit note. You should be able to get a cash refund or a replacement or a free repair. Unfortunately, it is not always such a cut-and-dried case, and exactly what you are entitled to may depend on how serious the fault is and how soon you tell the vendor about it. If you were told about the fault at the time, which may apply in the case of some sales goods, you have no right to return the goods. But generally speaking, buying in sales is no different from buying at any other time: you still have the full protection of the law.

You are not entitled to a refund if you change your mind about wanting to buy something, though some companies are generous in such circumstances and will allow you to exchange or be given a refund. Similarly, some shops are happy to exchange or allow credit on clothes that do not fit, but they must obviously still be unworn.

The rules cited above do not apply when you are buying goods privately. If the classified advertisement you answered was placed by a trader you are covered by the law, but in the case of a private transaction you can claim only if the goods are not as described. What you were told about the item's value and condition will be important, so if possible take someone with you when you go to look at the goods. If for example you bought a refrigerator that was said to be in good condition and when you got it home it would not work, you could claim your money back or the cost of repairing it. Pursuing such claims can, however, be costly, worrying and time-consuming, so try, particularly in the case of electrical goods, always to see the appliance working before you buy.

If you feel you are justified in your claim and you cannot get satisfaction from the shop you should go to a consumer advice centre to find out what to do next. Trading Standards Officers investigate false or misleading descriptions or prices, safety of goods and inaccurate weights and measures. Citizens' Advice Bureaux help with most complaints. If your concern is about food you should contact your local Environmental Health Officer.

If you have a problem with a 'service' such as a dry-cleaners, hairdressers or a travel agents you can still claim compensation if they did not carry out their task with reasonable care. Do not worry if the shop has a sign disclaiming responsibility for loss or damage however caused. This is known as an 'exclusion clause' and probably has no validity in law. Notices saying 'No money refunded' are illegal, too.

Guarantees are a useful bonus, but sometimes manufacturers try to limit their liability. Whatever the guarantee says, when something goes wrong with the item you can always claim your rights from the shop or company from which you bought it, provided it is still trading under the same management. (A frequent problem with guarantees which claim to last for years is that they may outlast the companies which issued them.)

WELFARE BENEFITS

If you have just left school or college you are not entitled to unemployment benefit because that is based on National Insurance contributions which you will not have paid. You may be entitled to supplementary benefit but you cannot claim it until the end of the school holidays after you leave. That means that if you leave at Easter you will only have to wait three weeks or so, but you will have a 6–7-week wait if you leave at the end of the summer term.

Supplementary benefit is means-tested, that is, to claim it you must provide details of any income or savings you may have. If you have more than £3,000 savings you will not be eligible, and if you earn more than £4 a week, the benefit will be deducted £ for £.

There are exceptions to this rule, so for full details ask for the leaflet NP12 at your Social Security office. It is called *Social Security, School-leavers and Students*, and it explains both what you pay and what you get.

School-leavers living with their parents can claim supplementary benefit. The amounts are increased each November. To receive this benefit you must be available for work and registered as unemployed at your local Unemployment Benefit office.

If you are at college or university you may apply for supplementary benefit in the holidays but not during term time.

If you are independent and want to sign on for supplementary benefit ask for form B1 at the Unemployment Benefit office.

If you have worked and paid Class I National Insurance contributions in the last complete tax year before the start of the tax year in which you are claiming, you may be entitled to unemployment benefit. You may be entitled to supplementary benefit as well, so claim for both. Leaflet NI12, *Unemployment Benefit*, will give you more information, including the current rates.

If you own or rent a house or flat, you may also be entitled to housing benefit, which is paid by local councils towards rent and general rates. (Other costs such as heating, lighting, hot water, etc. are in the province of the Social Security office.)

SIGNING ON

Do not delay signing on, as you will only receive benefit starting from the day on which you apply. As soon as you are unemployed or eligible for supplementary benefit go to the New Claims section of your nearest Unemployment Benefit office (look under 'Employment' in the phone book). If you are under 18 and a school-leaver, register with your local Careers Office before you go to sign on. When you leave employment you will be given a P45 form by your employer; take it with you to the Unemployment Benefit office. You also need to know your National Insurance number. (If you do not know it or have lost it, it can be traced.)

In the New Claims office you will be given a form, UB461, to fill in. If you have any difficulty filling it in ask for help. After that you will have to wait to be interviewed, not necessarily on the same day.

You will be asked at which post office you want to cash your Girocheque, as this is the way payments are normally made; you can only nominate one. Alternatively, you can pay the cheque in at a bank if you have a bank account.

You will receive a signing-on card, UB40, which tells you when you have to sign on next time and which queue to join when you arrive. If for any reason you cannot sign on let the office know in advance: you have to have a good reason not to keep to the appointed time – such as going for an interview, not just that you decided to go out for the day.

If you are claiming supplementary benefit you will have to fill in form B1 to take round to the local Social Security office. Do not forget to ask where this is. It will be quicker to take it round than post it.

Before you are granted supplementary benefit you will be interviewed and asked how much money you have, where you live, how much you pay for rent and rates or for board. If you live in a hotel or bed-and-breakfast accommodation your benefit will be made up of a weekly amount for the board and lodging and a personal allowance as well.

Do not forget that while you are on supplementary benefit you can claim free National Health Service dental treatment, spectacles and fares to hospital. Tell those concerned when you go for treatment that you are on supplementary benefit.

SEX AND THE LAW

It is against the law for a man or boy to have sex with a girl who is under 16, though a girl cannot be prosecuted for having sex under the age of consent.

If a girl has sex with her boyfriend before the age of 16 the police do not usually take any action unless the girl's parents complain. A girl who has already left home might be taken 'into care' (the local authority will appoint a social worker to look after her) on the grounds that she might be in moral danger. The social worker will decide where the girl should live: either at home, or perhaps in a community home, or with foster parents. Boys are very rarely taken into care unless they are thought to be having a homosexual relationship.

It is illegal for a man or boy to have a homosexual relationship until both are 21 years of age, though in a recent report the Policy Advisory Committee on Sexual Offences recommended that the minimum age for homosexual relationships between males should be reduced from 21 to 18.

CIGARETTE-SMOKING

You can smoke cigarettes in a private place at any age. You can be taken to court if you are between 10 and 16 and try to buy tobacco for your own use. It is also an offence to sell tobacco to anyone aged under 16.

If you are under 16 and are caught smoking in public a policeman or -woman may take the cigarettes away from you.

ALCOHOL

From the age of 5 you are allowed to drink alcohol on private premises.

From the age of 14 you can go into a public house, but may not drink alcohol there. When you are 16 you can drink beer, wine or cider with a meal in a hotel or restaurant. From the age of 18 you can drink in a pub and buy drinks there.

OWNING PROPERTY

You cannot own property in your own right until you are 18. If you are left land or property in a will and are under 18 it will normally be held in trust for you until you are of age. Different rules may apply abroad.

PASSPORTS

You need a passport to travel abroad. Under 16 you can travel on your parents' passport if travelling with them; after 16 you need your own regardless. You will need the consent of a parent to have a passport at 16 or under but at 18 you can get one whether or not your parents agree.

RIGHT TO VOTE

From the age of 18 you are entitled to vote in all government, European and local elections. If by 10 October in any year you have not received an electoral registration form, contact your local electoral registration officer at the local council offices to make sure your name is entered on the register. If, thereafter, you move house, you will have to go through the same routine again.

ADOPTION

If you were adopted, once you are 18 you have the right to see your birth records, which will tell you the name of one or both of your natural parents. Contact the Registrar of Births, Deaths and Marriages. If you were adopted before 12 November 1975 you will have to see a counsellor before you are shown your birth records.

MARRIAGE

At 16 you can marry with the consent of one parent or guardian. At 18 you can marry without your parents' consent.

EMERGENCY HELP

We all think emergencies only happen to other people, but unfortunately this is not so. Before trouble strikes, take time to make your own emergency help-list and pin it by the phone or somewhere else where you can refer to it easily.

Write down the phone number of your local police station, doctor and local hospital or nearest casualty department, together with the name and number of the area gas board (if you have gas) and a plumber with a 24-hour service. A few numbers for local mini-cab firms may also be useful.

STOLEN CREDIT CARDS

Tell the credit-card companies involved immediately your cards go missing. They run a 24-hour telephone service, so have the number written down and keep it in a different place from your cards, not in your handbag or diary, in case they are all stolen together.

Keep a note of your credit-card numbers at home too, together with the phone number to ring so that you can pass on the information as soon as possible.

SEXUAL ASSAULT OR RAPE
You will need someone to talk to, a friend to help you through the shock. If you decide to report the matter to the police, do so at once before you change your clothes or wash. In any case you should see a doctor as soon as possible to check for VD, injury or pregnancy. The Rape Crisis Centre provides a 24-hour help line and can give you emotional as well as practical support. See also Chapter 9.

POLICE RIGHTS
If you are driving a car and are stopped by police you are legally obliged to give your name and address.

Should you be stopped in the street by police you are not obliged to say anything, but it is as well to be courteous and give your name and address if asked. If they ask simple questions such as 'Where are you going?' or 'Where have you been?' it is sensible to answer, but if the questioning goes on you should ask why you are being questioned and if you wish may decline to answer any more questions.

If you have been a witness to an incident such as an accident you can be asked by the police to give your name and address as a possible witness; if the police suspect you of withholding evidence when you have been witness to a crime, you may be arrested.

There are a number of situations in which the police can stop you and search you: under the new Police and Criminal Evidence legislation the police will have vastly increased powers to stop and search you if they suspect you have committed a criminal offence.

It is best to agree to a search, but ask why, and ask whether you are being arrested.

If you agree to be searched and you are in the street you can ask to be searched in private at a police station. Unless you have been arrested, once you have been searched you are free to go.

FIRE
If you discover a fire at home get everyone out of the room and close the door. Make everyone leave the building and call the fire brigade by dialling 999.

Clothes on fire   Lie down and roll across the floor. If you can wrap yourself in a rug or blanket, so much the better, but do not waste time looking for something. Get medical help at once as you will be suffering from shock and probably burns as well.

Chip pan/frying-pan fire   Turn off the heat and cover the flames with the lid of the pan if there is one, or a tin tray or a thick damp cloth. Do not put water on the pan or try to carry it outside.

Oil stove   Do not attempt to move it. Cover it with a damp rug or large towel. Close the door of the room to minimize the draught. Call the fire brigade if you cannot deal with it and make everyone leave the house.

FROZEN CAR LOCK

If you cannot get into your car on a cold frosty night, your lock is probably frozen up. For best protection, keep de-icer in the house as well as in the car. Failing that, breathe into the lock (without letting your lips touch the metal) or pour lukewarm water over it.

LOCKED OUT

It is a good idea to leave a key with a trusted friend who lives nearby, or with a neighbour. Do not mark it with your address in case *they* have burglars, but do agree between you where it will be kept. It is *not* a good idea to have a spare key in a flower-pot or under the mat. The burglar will get to it before you.

If you cannot gain entry to the house because you have forgotten your key, do not risk life and limb by trying to climb into an upstairs window without proper equipment. Ask the police if they can help you. Even if they cannot they will have the name of a locksmith, but you will need proof of identity.

DESPAIR

Sometimes unhappiness or depression can seem to be overwhelming and you will need some immediate positive help. Talking to someone who will not be upset or shocked by what you have to say and who will have time to listen can help considerably.

The Samaritans offer a 24-hour telephone line to offer advice to those who feel they cannot cope with life. Their phone number is in every telephone directory.

Reference

Chapter 2 FINDING SOMEWHERE TO LIVE

Housing
SHAC, The London Housing Aid Centre, 189a Old Brompton Road, London, SW5 0AR; tel. 01-373 7841 or 01-373 7276.
SHELTER (National Campaign for the Homeless), 157 Waterloo Road, London, SE1 8XF; tel. 01-633 9377.
Regional centres:
Birmingham: 177 Corporation Street, Birmingham, B4 6RG; tel. 021 236 6668.
Bristol: Dunns Buildings, Thomas Lane, Bristol, BS1 6JG; tel. 0272 281151.
Leeds: Charlton House, 36 Hunslet Road, Leeds, LS10 1JN; tel. 0532 451460.
Leicester: 13 Welford Road, Leicester; tel. 0533 546064.
Manchester: Room 239, 2nd floor, Corn Exchange Buildings, Manchester, M4 3BP; tel. 061 834 4809.
Newbury: 9 Cromwell Place, Newbury, Berks, RG13 1AF; tel. 0635 45205.
Newcastle: 33 Groatmarket, Newcastle-on-Tyne; tel. 0632 23778.
Plymouth: Resources Centre, Virginia House, Palace Street, Plymouth; tel. 0752 21187.
Sandwell: 2 Church Square, Oldbury, Sandwell; tel. 021 552 2339.
Taunton: Cattlemoat Chambers, Corporation Street, Taunton, Somerset; tel. 0823 52037.
Welwyn: 75 Haldens, Welwyn Garden City, Herts; AL7 1DH; tel. Welwyn 20001.
Shelter Wales: 57 Walter Road, Swansea; tel. 0792 469400.
Shelter Scotland:
   Edinburgh: 6 Castle Street, Edinburgh, EH2 3AT; tel. 031 226 6347.
   Aberdeen: St Katherine's Centre, 5 West North Street, Aberdeen; tel. 0224 53586.
   Edinburgh: 25 Frederick Street, Edinburgh 8; tel. 031 225 6058.
   Glasgow: 53 St Vincent Crescent, Glasgow 3; tel. 041 221 8995.

Shelter Northern Ireland:
  Belfast: 16 Howard Street, Belfast, BT1 6PA; tel. 0232 47752.
  Omagh: 2 John Street, Omagh, Co. Tyrone, N. Ireland; tel.
  0662 44985.
FIRST KEY, for young people leaving care: Hatley House, Green
Walk, London, SE1 4TV.
NATIONAL ASSOCIATION FOR ASIAN YOUTH runs a single
girls' hostel in Southall, Middx. and offers counselling and
advice. Head Office: 46 High Street, Southall, Middx., UB1 3DB;
tel. 01-574 1325/6/7.
HOUSING ADVICE SWITCHBOARD, 47 Charing Cross Road,
London, WC2H 0AN; tel. 01-434 2522.
ADVISORY SERVICE FOR SQUATTERS, 2 Pauls Road,
London, N1; tel. 01-359 8814.
HOME BASE, 157 Waterloo Road, London, SE1 8XF; tel. 01-
633 9377.
CAMPAIGN FOR SINGLE HOMELESS PEOPLE (CHAR), 5–15
Cromer Street, London, WC1H 2LS; tel. 01-833 2071.
DORA JESSOP SHELTERING HOME FOR GIRLS, for
temporary shelter and counselling, 34 Sunny Bank, Hull; tel.
Hull 42740.
ALONE IN LONDON service (formerly G.A.L.S.), provides
accommodation for homeless, destitute or workless young
people, also counselling and information: West Lodge, 190
Euston Road, London, NW1 2EF; tel. 01-387 3010.
YMCA, provides accommodation for over 8000 young people
throughout Britain, sometimes overnight accommodation but
mainly for longer stays: 640 Forest Road, London, E17 3DZ; tel.
01-520 5599.
YWCA, has 82 different residences throughout England, Wales
and Scotland; for more details write to 2 Weymouth Street,
London, W1N 4AX; tel. 01-631 0657.

Advice only
BROMLEY Y, counselling agency for young people: 17 Ethelbert
Road, Bromley, Kent, BR1 1JA; tel. 01-464 9033.
SOHO PROJECT, 142 Charing Cross Road, London, WC2H
0LB; tel. 01-836 8121.
PICCADILLY ADVICE CENTRE, Subway Four, Piccadilly
Circus Underground Station, London, W1; tel. 01-930 0066.
CENTREPOINT EMERGENCY HOSTEL, 65a Shaftesbury
Avenue, London, W1; tel. 01-734 1075.
RIVERPOINT EMERGENCY HOSTEL, 229 King Street,
Hammersmith, London, W6; tel. 01-734 2888.
CAMDEN RESETTLEMENT UNIT, 4 Birkenhead Street,

London, WC1 (opposite Kings Cross Station); tel. 01-278 6466.
BASEMENT YOUTH PROJECT, 227 Earls Court Road, London, SW5; tel. 01-373 2335.
NATIONAL FEDERATION OF 18-PLUS GROUPS has over 200 groups that meet throughout Britain. Good places to meet people. Write to head office to find nearest group to you: 18-PLUS, Nicholson House, Old Court Road, Newent, Glos, GL18 1AG; tel. Newent 821210.
ASSOCIATION FOR JEWISH YOUTH, Aju House, 50 Lindley Street, London, E1 3AX; tel. 01-790 6407.
OPEN DOOR, Hornsey Young People's Consultation Service, 12 Middle Lane, Crouch End, Hornsey, London, N8 8PL; tel. 01-348 5947.

Short-life housing
London: contact Housing Advice Switchboard or SHAC (see above). In other areas contact the local council or a housing advice centre.

Gay flat-shares
GAY SWITCHBOARD, runs an accommodation service for gays: London tel. 01-837 7324.

Chapter 3   GETTING YOUR PLACE TOGETHER

Reading an electricity meter
Being able to read a meter means you can check it when you first take over a flat or house and also keep an eye on the number of units you are consuming. To get a rough idea of how much you are using each week, read the meter every week at roughly the same time. Then you will know how big a bill you are running up and whether you should start to make some savings by using the electric fire less frequently or rationing the hot water used for baths.

There are two types of meter, the dial type and the cyclometer type. Each registers ten thousands, thousands, hundreds, tens and single units (kilowatt hours or kWh).

kWh is 1000 watts (1kW) used continuously for one hour and known as the unit. Your local electricity board (or the previous bill) will tell you how much you are being charged per unit.

On a dial type meter, you will see that the hands on adjacent dials revolve in opposite directions. Begin at either end and write down the figures indicated in sequence. When the hand is between two figures write down the lower figure. When the hand is between 0 and 9 write down 9. When the hand is on a figure (say 7) write down 6 unless the hand on the next dial on the right is between 0 and 1. Disregard the smaller dial registering tenths of a unit, since this is used mainly for testing purposes.

Once you have taken the meter readings over a two- or three-week period you will have some idea of the number of units you are consuming each week.

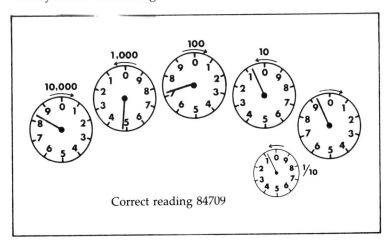

Correct reading 84709

The other type of meter is the cyclometer type, which is read straight off like a car milometer.

(Diagrams reproduced by courtesy of The Electrical Association for Women)

Useful addresses
BATHROOM IDEAS BUREAU, 44 Earlham Street, London, WC2; tel. 01-240 0959.

BATHROOM AND SHOWER CENTRE, 204 Great Portland Street, London, W1; tel. 01-388 7631.
CARPET MANUFACTURERS' ASSOCIATION, 26 St James Square, London, SW1; tel. 01-839 2145.
ELECTRICAL ASSOCIATION FOR WOMEN, Write for leaflets. Open daily for free advice on domestic electricity. One-day courses are held: 25 Fouberts Place, London, W1V 2AL; tel. 01-437 5212.
ELECTRICITY COUNCIL, 30 Millbank, London, SW1P 4RD; tel. 01-834 2333.
BRITISH GAS, Rivermill House, 152 Grosvenor Road, London, SW1V 3JL; tel. 01-821 1444.
BRITISH LIGHTING COUNCIL, c/o F. Radford Ltd, 38 Charlotte Street, London, W1P 1HP; tel. 01-637 9792.
BRITISH SAFETY COUNCIL, 62–64 Chancellor's Road, London, W6; tel. 01-741 1231.
GLASS AND GLAZING FEDERATION, 6 Mount Row, London, W1Y 6DY; tel. 01-629 8334.
HOME LAUNDERING CONSULTATIVE COUNCIL, Wellington House, 6–9 Upper St Martin's Lane, London, WC2H 9DL; tel. 01-836 4545.
MICROWAVE OVEN ASSOCIATION, 16a The Broadway, London, SW19; tel. 01-946 3389.
RENTOKIL LTD, Felcourt, East Grinstead, West Sussex, RH19 2JY; tel. 0342 833022.

Chapter 4 A JOB WITH A FUTURE

Useful addresses
NATIONAL ADVISORY CENTRE ON CAREERS FOR WOMEN, Drayton House, 30 Gordon Street, London, WC1H 0AX.
CAREERS RESEARCH AND ADVISORY CENTRE (CRAC), Bateman Street, Cambridge, CB2 1LZ.
CAREERS AND OCCUPATIONAL INFORMATION CENTRE (COIC), Room W1101, Moor Foot, Sheffield, S1 4PQ.
BUSINESS EDUCATION COUNCIL, Berkshire House, 168–173 High Holborn, London, WC1V 7AG.
SCOTTISH BUSINESS EDUCATION COUNCIL, 22 Great King Street, Edinburgh, EH3 6QH.
BUSINESS AND TECHNICIAN EDUCATION COUNCIL, Central House, Upper Woburn Place, London, WC1H 0HH.
SCOTTISH TECHNICAL EDUCATION COUNCIL, 38 Queen's Street, Glasgow, G1 3DY.

Vocational guidance
CAREERS ANALYSTS, Career House, 90 Gloucester Place, London, W1H 4BL.
VOCATIONAL GUIDANCE ASSOCIATION, 7 Harley House, Upper Harley Street, London, NW1 4RP.
Both can quote an impressive list of success stories from people of all ages. Write for free brochure.

Jobfinder service
Capital Radio Jobmate, National Extension College, 8 Strutton Ground, London, SW1 2HP; tel. 01-222 0222. There are also staff on hand in the foyer of Capital Radio, Euston Tower, London, NW1 during weekdays, 9.30 am–4 pm; tel. 01-439 2222.

Career opportunities
Animal nursing
Animal nursing auxiliaries work with veterinary surgeons in their practices. They tend animals in the vet's care, remove stitches, assist in animals' post-operative care and generally help the vet in his practice.

Two examinations must be passed before you can be registered by the Royal College of Veterinary Surgeons: one which can be taken any time after your enrolment as a trainee, and a final examination which can be taken not less than nine months afterwards. The syllabus covers mainly the dog and cat but you will gain some knowledge of other small animals such as rabbits, hamsters, mice and caged birds. Before being accepted by the Royal College of Veterinary Surgeons for enrolment as a trainee you must have a job at a practice that is an approved training centre, or the written offer of such employment.

Training is on the job and supplemented by courses of part-time study. Some full-time courses are available at agricultural colleges, which count as part of a two-year training programme.

To be accepted as a trainee you need passes in four O-levels at A, B or C grade, or Grade 1 CSE, including a pass in English language and a pass in either a physical or biological science or in mathematics.

For a leaflet send a large s.a.e. to the Royal College of Veterinary Surgeons, 32 Belgrave Square, London, SW1X 8QP.

Beauty therapy
To qualify as a general beauty therapist you can either take a course sponsored by the City and Guilds of London Institute,

the International Health and Beauty Council or the Confederation of Beauty Therapy and Cosmetology; or you can apply to a technical college or a private school (of which there are many). The minimum age for most courses is about 17½, but for one or two you need only be 16. If you take a course at a local education authority college you may qualify for a grant.

The range of jobs for beauty therapists is wide. You can work in a department store as a beauty consultant selling cosmetics, or in the beauty department of a hairdressing salon; you could work on board a cruise ship or run your own visiting beauty practice, attending clients in their own homes.

A more specialized training would enable you to practise electrolysis or as a remedial camouflage therapist, counselling people in the art of make-up to disguise scars, including accident scars. For this you would probably work within the dermatology department of a hospital plastic surgery department.

Figure correction is another important area – the fastest-growing section of the industry.

Beauticians also work in TV studios and as freelance make-up artists with models at photographic sessions; a high degree of imagination and professionalism is required for such jobs. Finally, if you can combine a beauty training with a flair for words you could join the elite band of journalists who write about all aspects of beauty for women's magazines.

For more details of training write to the City and Guilds of London Institute, 46 Britannia Street, London, WC1X 9RG; the International Health and Beauty Council, PO Box 36, Arundel, West Sussex, BN18 0SW; the Confederation of Beauty Therapy and Cosmetology, 6 Hillside Gardens, Spinney Hill, Addlestone, Surrey, KT15 1AX; or the British Association of Electrolysists, 6 Quakers Mede, Haddenham, Bucks, HP17 8EB.

Catering and hotel work
The range of jobs is vast: bar staff, waiter/waitress, chefs, receptionists, snack-bar staff, hotel housekeeping and general management positions – all come within the general scope of catering.

There are two sides to the industry: the hotel/restaurant area and the service and welfare field, which includes catering in hospitals, canteens, schools.

Some jobs require in-house training and few technical qualifications. The City and Guilds of London Institute offers various 'Specific Skill' schemes, such as Food Service Assistant and Counter Service Assistant.

A number of part-time courses are run for bar staff and publicans by the Licensed Trade Training and Education Committee, the Brewers' Society and the Hotel and Catering Industry Training Board, in addition to the City and Guilds of London's specific skill scheme for bar staff.

At management level you could qualify for the BTEC Certificate and Higher Certificate or the BTEC (SCOTEC in Scotland) diplomas and certificates, for which you need O-levels (or CSE Grade 1) and sometimes A-levels, depending on the course chosen

For further details ask your careers officer (also about opportunities in this field under the Youth Training Scheme) or write to: Business and Technician Education Council, Central House, Upper Woburn Place, London, WC1H 0HH; or Scottish Technical Education Council, 38 Queen's Street, Glasgow, G1 3DY; Hotel Catering and Institutional Management Association Courses, 191 Trinity Road, London, SW17 7HN; The Brewers' Society, Retail Training Dept., 42 Portman Square, London, W1H 0BB; Wine and Spirit Education Trust, Five Kings House, Kennet Wharf Lane, Upper Thames Street, London, EC4U 3AJ; and the Hotel and Catering Industry Training Board, PO Box 18, Ramsey House, Central Square, Wembley, Middx, HA9 7AP, which has regional offices at 10 Magdala Crescent, Edinburgh; Prudential Building, Wine Street, Bristol; The Graftons, Stamford New Road, Altrincham; Stonebow House, The Stonebow, York; Ansvar House, 31 St Leonards Road, Eastbourne; Old Courts, All Saints Road, Newmarket (these branches also have 24-hour answering services; see telephone directory).

Many large hotel chains and restaurants do their own in-house training, so if there is one particular one that interests you, write to its head office or ask at a local branch of the chain. For further details write to Business and Technician Education Council, Central House, Upper Woburn Place, London, WC1H 0HH; Scottish Technical Education Council, 38 Queen's Street, Glasgow, G1 3DY.

Civil Service
The Civil Service is the biggest employer of office workers in the country and the scope of jobs is equally wide. It includes Inland Revenue departments, DHSS offices, museums and Jobcentres, to name just a few.

Basic entry is normally as a Clerical Assistant, for which two GCE O-levels or the equivalent are needed, or Clerical Officer, for which 5 O-levels or the equivalent are necessary. If you have

149

two GCE A-levels and 3 O-levels you can apply for a post as Executive Officer, with responsibility of applying departmental policy, seeing jobs are done properly by others or doing basic background work, perhaps for a senior civil servant.

Salaries are paid on a set scale and normally rise annually. Promotion prospects are generally good.

Graduates have an equally wide range of jobs open to them in terms of both general management and administration and also in specialist careers such as engineering, science or economics.

Two booklets are available free: *Civil Service Careers GCE/CSE Level* and *Civil Service Careers, Degree Level*.

Junior jobs are generally recruited at local level. Ask at your Jobcentre, write to the Establishment Officer at departments in your area or ask your careers adviser for more details. Alternatively, write to the Civil Service Commission, Alencon Link, Basingstoke, Hampshire, RG21 1JB.

Computing

The computer industry has mushroomed recently and for qualified people is still one of the more fertile job-hunting grounds.

The number of jobs available varies enormously from area to area, so ask your careers officer or the local Jobcentre what the possibilities are like locally before you undertake training.

The three main types of job that you could do straight from school are VDU operation/data preparation, data control and computer operating. VDU is a keyboard job for which typing is a good preparation. A data control department receives from other departments documents to be processed. For computer operating you usually need several O- and sometimes A-levels, usually in mathematics or English. You need to be able to use machinery and work carefully, and there is often shift work.

Programming is the next step, for which employers usually require O-levels, particularly in mathematics and English, and several A-levels (or Scottish Higher Grade passes).

Maintenance engineering is another aspect of computer work, for which you need a clean driving licence and at least a National Diploma or Certificate in some branch of engineering. TV repair experience could be relevant.

Look for companies that operate their own training schemes. Treat computer schools with caution. Ask how many applicants they turn down as unsuitable for training, how many students they place in jobs after the course, how many get jobs and at what salaries. Enquire whether the school complies with the NCC Code of Practice for commercial computer schools.

Some universities offer directly relevant courses such as electronic engineering or physics for hardware design and computer science for systems programming. Degree courses at polytechnics and universities are listed in *Degree Course Guide: Computer Science*, published by Hobsons Press for the Careers Research and Advisory Centre.

The National Computing Centre publishes guides for school-leavers, potential graduates and those interested in a career switch to computing. Write to the Centre at Oxford Road, Manchester, M1 7ED.

Driving instruction
Apart from having held a full licence for four years and being a skilled driver, you must be calm and patient and genuinely enjoy teaching. To be a trainee driving instructor you need a licence from the Department of Transport and within a year you must pass a stringent test including a written examination plus practical tests of your own driving and instructional ability.

You may find a driving school that will take you on as a trainee driving instructor. The Motor Schools Association of G.B. Ltd offers training courses through their network of tutors at various centres around Britain. Courses generally last for two weeks. Before they accept you they will test your own driving so that if there is a basic flaw you will not waste money being trained. They reject 8–9 out of every 10 applicants as unsuitable.

Once qualified it is often simplest to work through an established local driving school as a self-employed person. This gives you the protection of a known name and the advantages of group advertising. Pay can be good but expenses are very high. You will pay a certain amount of money each week to the school to cover the cost of hire of the car, insurance, tax, servicing and repairs. You pay for petrol yourself. Hours are unsocial (mainly evenings and weekends).

Enquire at your local driving schools or write to the Chief Training Officer, The Motor Schools Association, 11 Kenyon Street, Manchester, M18 8SH.

Hairdressing
There are three ways of becoming a hairdresser:
(1) A 3-year training apprenticeship at a salon. This incorporates day release to local authority training courses. The advantages are that you can learn on the job and receive a small wage during training. At the end you take a City and Guilds of London (or regional equivalent) examination.
(2) A local authority or polytechnic or college hairdressing

course. This takes 2 years and you may be able to supplement the training with Saturday work in a local salon. You take a City and Guilds examination (or regional equivalent) at the end.

(3) A training course at a hairdressing school. Most beginners' courses are for about 6 months and provide basic knowledge, but they are not as well regarded as the apprenticeship or the 2-year course. For more information or a list of schools and fees write to the National Hairdressers' Federation, 11 Goldington Road, Bedford, or the Guild of Hairdressers, 24 Woodbridge Road, Guildford, Surrey.

Stamina is the most important quality for a hairdresser as the hours are long and standing all day is tiring. You need to be skilful with your hands, patient and like meeting people – even difficult customers. Types of salon range from small local shops to salons in the West End, in hotels and on board ship.

Home economics
The following qualifications are recognized by the Institute of Home Economics: B.Sc. and B.A. at ordinary and honours level; degree courses in education at ordinary and honours level with a speciality in home economics; BTEC Higher Diploma in home economics; BTEC Diploma in home economics; City and Guilds of London Institute (794) Certificate in Home Economics for Family and Community Care (accepted as a non-corporate category of affiliation); BTEC National Diploma or Higher National Diploma. All these are either 2- or 3-year courses.

The scope for work as a home economist is wide. Jobs range from working in the fuel industries (for the Gas or Electricity Boards), giving advice to consumers and undertaking promotional work. Home economists are sometimes retained by retail stores such as supermarkets and freezer shops as well as within the manufacturing industry.

Advertising, public relations companies and magazines employ home economists and work ranges from evaluating equipment and writing leaflets to devising recipes. At the top of the tree you might work as a self-employed freelance for photographers specializing in food, or preparing food for commercials; or you could write textbooks or general cookery books yourself.

A B.Ed. degree prepares home economists to teach in secondary, further and higher education.

The Institute of Home Economics issues a salary guide, though there is no nationally recognized salary scale. It is increasingly difficult to gain entry into the field without experience, but, once in, the prospects of advancement are good.

For further information write to colleges and polytechnics offering courses in home economics: City and Guilds of London Institute, 46 Britannia Street, London, WC1X 9RG; Business and Technician Education Council, Central House, Upper Woburn Place, London, WC1H 0HH; and the Institute of Home Economics Ltd, 2nd floor, 192/198 Vauxhall Bridge Road, London, SW1V 1DX.

Market research

A comparatively new industry, market research involves providing information which tests the potential market for products or services. Face-to-face street interviews are only one aspect: there is likely to be considerably more work at a desk or interviewing on the telephone, or analysing complicated data.

Companies requiring market researchers are more likely to want graduates, perhaps in business studies or psychology or social science, though other disciplines would be acceptable for someone with the right approach.

You will need to enjoy solving problems, have the ability to express yourself well and be able to deal with people at all levels.

You might find yourself working for a market research agency, or for the market research department of an industrial company or an advertising agency or a government department.

Field work could mean working part-time under the guidance of a field manager, working evenings and weekends visiting people in their homes, or setting up meetings in local halls to which the public is invited to come and voice opinions on products or take part in discussion groups.

Most market researchers take up membership of the Market Research Society, which also runs a diploma scheme.

For more details write to the Education Office, Market Research Society, 15 Belgrave Square, London, SW1X 8PF; or the Industrial Marketing Research Association, 11 Bird Street, Lichfield, Staffs.

Nursing

The most important requirement for anyone wishing to become a nurse is to want to care for people, which means talking and listening to them, being concerned for their overall welfare and giving support to their relatives, as well as tending to their physical needs as patients.

There are two main qualifications: Enrolled Nurse (General) or second-level nurse (previously known as State Enrolled Nurse) and Registered General Nurse or first-level nurse (previously known as State Registered Nurse). Those who qualified before 1 July 1983 will keep their original titles, but new nurses will assume the new titles.

A minimum of 5 O-levels is required for acceptance to train as a RGN, including English language and a science subject. To train as an Enrolled Nurse you need a minimum of 2 O-levels or CSE Grade 1 passes, including English.

If you hope to do a combined degree/registration course your choice of O- and A-level subjects is very important: write for advice to the Universities Central Council for Admissions (UCCA), PO Box 28, Cheltenham, Glos, GL50 1HY.

Courses range in duration from 98 or 146 weeks plus annual leave and statutory holidays. Combined degree/registration courses generally take at least 4 years.

Once qualified, most nurses work with the National Health Service. After initial training and some general experience there are many opportunities to specialize in the fields of, for example, child nursing, nursing the mentally handicapped or mentally ill, midwifery and community nursing (to name just a few). You can also train to nurse the mentally ill without taking the general nursing course.

Advice and information can be obtained by writing to the Nursing and Health Service Careers Centre, 121/123 Edgware Road, London, W2 2HX.

For more details look at *Where Do I Go from Here? Career opportunities for registered nurses* (booklet NLO 40, from the DHSS).

For details of nursing training in Scotland write to the Scottish Health Service, Crewe Road South, Edinburgh, EH4 2LF. In Wales, write to the Welsh Office, Information Division, Crown Office, Cathays Park, Cardiff, CF1 3NQ. In Northern Ireland: the National Board for Nursing, Midwifery and Health Visiting for Northern Ireland, RAC House, 79 Chichester Street, Belfast, BT1 4JE.

Physiotherapy

Physiotherapy is a mentally and physically challenging career. Candidates need to be extremely fit, and anyone under 158 cm (5 feet 2 inches), or over-tall might not be accepted: small people might not be able to inspire the necessary confidence into immobile patients they have to lift, while over-tall students might be prone to back trouble.

Physiotherapists use their special training to help patients who are injured or physically disabled to achieve as near normal an active life as possible. They need not only to be skilled but to be able to establish a rapport with patients and instil into them the desire to get better. Perseverance and tact are essential, as well as the ability to be kind but firm on occasion.

Students should be 18 years of age by 1 November of the year they begin training, though this can be waived if they have the necessary entry qualifications. These are a minimum of 7 GCE subjects, of which at least two must be at A-level. O-level grades must be A, B or C. English and 2 science subjects are compulsory. The alternative Scottish Certificate of Education requires 7 specified subjects, at least three of which must be at the Higher Grade, and at least 2 science subjects are required.

The approved diploma or degree qualification leads to membership of the Chartered Society of Physiotherapy. Courses last for three (sometimes four) academic years, full time, and include practical as well as academic study.

Most physiotherapists work within the Health Service and are employed in hospitals. However, they also work in schools and with the mentally and physically handicapped. Some work in industry and there are some posts in sport. It is possible to go into full-time or part-time practice.

For more details send an s.a.e. to the Central Admissions Dept., Chartered Society of Physiotherapy, 14 Bedford Row, London, WC1R 4ED.

Police

To join the police you must be physically fit, a British or Commonwealth subject and 'of good character'. You should also be at least 168 cm (5 feet 6 inches) tall if you are a woman, 172 cm (5 feet 8 inches) tall if you are a man. You also need self-confidence, initiative, common sense and a desire to serve the community. The minimum age for acceptance as a recruit is 18½, but before that you could apply to become a police cadet.

Conditions vary considerably within the police forces and especially between those in rural or city areas.

Once accepted you will have two years as a police constable on probation. During the two years you will receive an extremely thorough practical as well as theoretical training to enable you to meet the extremely varied problems and conditions you will meet in the job. After that you may decide to go into one of the specialist branches such as CID or Special Branch.

Promotion up to Inspector is by examination and selection; after that, by selection only.

For further information write to the Chief Constable of any police force; in the metropolitan area write to the Metropolitan Police, Careers Information and Selection Centre, 6 Harrow Road, London, W2 1XH.

Public relations
Public relations work appears to be one of the growth industries, although it is extremely difficult to break into without any previous experience. The scope of public relations work is wide. It covers government departments, nationalized industries and charities as well as the wide spectrum of private industry. You may be promoting a person, a project, fund-raising or a specific product.

The work is complex and varied and might range from political lobbying to writing and sending out leaflets to school-leavers and arranging for the photography of products. You may be the liaison between management and staff in a large company by means of a house journal. You could be asked to arrange press conferences or organize newspaper competitions or talk to women's groups about the firms you represent.

Basically you will work either on the staff of a company, a government department, a local authority or in a consultancy which may have a number of clients.

Qualities needed will include the ability to communicate, in both writing and speech. You will need imagination to work out new ways of promoting what may be an old idea or a traditional product. You must be methodical and able to manage a budget. You will have to be prepared to work long hours and under pressure when necessary.

You may be able to get a foot on the ladder by starting work as a secretary or general assistant in a large PR department. Some firms accept graduate trainees. Many public relations officers have previously been journalists.

Qualifications vary, but most firms will expect you to have one or two A-levels. Training is mostly on the job but you can study part-time for a CAM Diploma. For more details write to the Communications, Advertising and Marketing Foundation, Abford House, 15 Wilton Road, London, SW1V 1NJ.

For more information write to the Institute of Public Relations, Gate House, St John's Square, London, EC1M 4DH.

Retailing and distribution
The choice of careers within retailing and distribution is as

different as the types of goods sold. It can range from working in a local shop or large department store to a supermarket, warehouse or with a mail order company.

There are opportunities for people with no academic qualifications to work up from the bottom provided they have aptitude and a suitable personality. There are also openings for those with CSE or O-level passes and A-level or graduate qualifications.

Promotion can be rapid, although nowadays more attention is given to studying for additional qualifications within a particular trade. Many large companies have their own training schemes.

For a selling career you should enjoy meeting people and be able to establish a rapport with them quickly. You will certainly need stamina, especially in the early part of your career when you may spend most of your time on your feet. You should also be methodical, and it helps if you are numerate as you may have to check stock.

To become a buyer you will have to acquire detailed knowledge of 'your' commodity: this will be mostly on the job, though extra study may be required. Buyers often handle a budget of millions of pounds, though in small businesses the owner and manager will do his own buying. In some spheres you need to have a flair for knowing what the public will want before they know themselves (if you work in the fast-changing world of fashion, for example).

For the best prospects look at the chain stores or the large department stores where you can specialize in one area of the business, such as do-it-yourself, china and glass or knitting yarns. If you have a particular skill or interest you may prefer to work in a smaller shop that specializes, in which case you may eventually have to cover a wider range of activities such as accounts, selling to the public, buying merchandise and managing staff.

Trainee managers are likely to be recruited from among those with A-levels or degrees, although it is still possible to become a manager without any qualifications and to have on-the-job training supplemented by part-time study.

The Business Education Council has a series of courses suitable for a career in retailing. In Scotland, enquire about the SCOTBEC Certificate (SNC and SHNC) in distribution studies. Part-time day and/or evening courses are available at colleges throughout Britain.

You could also enquire about TOPS schemes if you fulfil other TOPS requirements (see Chapter 11).

Write for more information to the British Retailers

Association, Commonwealth House, 1-19 New Oxford Street, London, WC1A 1PA; Business Education Council, Berkshire House, 168–173 High Holborn, London, WC1V 7AG; Scottish Business Education Council, 22 Great King Street, Edinburgh, EH3 6QH.

Social work

Social workers help people to cope with their lives and to sort out their personal and social problems. The people in their care may be under great stress or in trouble with the law, and will be from a wide variety of social backgrounds. Even if the circumstances cannot be altered, as in the case of a mental or physical infirmity, social workers can help people come to terms with their disabilities and counsel them so that they can lead as full a life within the community as possible.

Social workers may be attached to the local social services department and meet their clients at the offices or in their own homes. They may work from day centres, hospitals or health centres, or in child guidance centres or residential homes.

A career in social work may be entered at various levels. If you have no or few qualifications you can leave school at 16 with a view to taking a 2-year, full-time course leading to the Preliminary Certificate in Social Care. This does not give you any qualification but gives you a valuable insight into the services and whether you could fit in. It also helps you to gain some experience while you continue your education, as you would be encouraged to study for extra O-levels. Practical work is combined with further education. Ask your Careers Officer about the course run by the Central Council for Education and Training in Social Work (CCETSW).

If you are 20 years of age you can start to train for a non-graduate course. You will need at least 5 O-levels, including English or Welsh, and in England, Wales or Northern Ireland preferably 2 GCE A-levels. In Scotland the normal requirements are two SCE O-levels and three SCE Higher Grades or their equivalent; one pass must be in English. Leaflet 2 from CCETSW has the relevant information.

If you plan to study for a degree a number of universities or polytechnics offer a 4-year social science degree course with an option in social work.

Alternatively you can take a relevant social science degree course followed by a one-year course leading to the Certificate of Qualification in Social Work (CQSW). Yet another option is to take a non-relevant degree course followed by a 2-year post-graduate social work course leading to the CQSW. Ask for information sheets 2 and 18 from CCETSW.

Apart from being a social worker you could investigate the back-up jobs available within the various agencies such as clerical or domestic, or specialist services for the mentally or physically handicapped.

You may be able to train for the Certificate in Social Service (CSS) (details from CCETSW Information Service).

The leaflet *Looking After People* describes other caring and helping jobs; it is available from the Dept. of Education and Science, Room 1/27, Elizabeth House, York Road, London, SE1 7HP (or ask for it at your careers office).

There are also opportunities in youth and community work: see information sheets from CCETSW or write to the National Youth Bureau, 17–23 Albion Street, Leicester, LE1 6GD, or the Scottish Community Education Council, Atholl House, 2 Canning Street, Edinburgh, EH3 8EG, the Council for Education and Training in Youth and Community Work, Wellington House, Wellington Street, Leicester, LE1 6HL, or the Youth Welfare Branch of the Dept. of Education (Northern Ireland), Rathgael House, Balloo Road, Bangor, Co. Down, BR19 2PR.

Your careers officer may have these leaflets already.

The CCETSW may be contacted at its Central Office, Derbyshire House, St Chad's Street, London, WC1H 8AD; or at West Wing, St David's House, Wood Street, Cardiff, CF1 1ES; at 9 South St David's Street, Edinburgh, EH2 2BW; or at 14 Malone Road, Belfast, BT9 5BN.

Chapter 6 MANAGING MONEY

Cheques

There are two types of cheque, crossed (with two parallel lines across) and open (without the lines). An open cheque can be cashed by the payee (the person to whom payment is being made) at the branch of the bank upon which the cheque was drawn, but a crossed cheque can only be paid into a bank account.

Most people operate with crossed cheques, which are less vulnerable to fraud – especially important for those sent through the post.

When you write a cheque, get into the habit of writing the counterfoil first so that you always have a record of how much you have paid out and to whom. Then write the date (banks will not pay on cheques dated ahead), the payee's name against the word 'Pay', the amount payable, on the line below in both words and figures, and sign with your usual signature. Check that the payee's name is spelt correctly, and that initials, if used, are correct. If you want to draw cash yourself just write the word 'cash' or 'self' on the line after 'Pay'. Strictly speaking, you should write 'pay cash' between the parallel lines as well. Where you have entered the amount, make sure that the words and figures agree and that you have not left space where extra words or figures could be added.

Note that cheques can be stopped by the drawer – the person who issued the cheque – unless they were issued in conjunction with a cheque guarantee card or have already been cleared. The bank's fee for stopping a cheque ranges from £2 to £5.

If a cheque is written when there is insufficient in the account to cover the amount, the bank may return the cheque unpaid (R/D, refer to drawer), but cannot do this if it was issued with a cheque guarantee card. In this case the bank may request the return of the card and the cheque book.

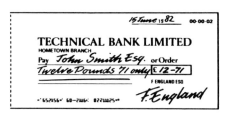

Further advice on banking
ACCESS, Access House, Southend-on-Sea, SS2 6QQ; tel. 0702 352255.
VISA/BARCLAYCARD, Dept. MU, 72 Northampton, NN1 1SG; tel. 0604 21100.
NATIONAL GIROBANK, Bootle, Merseyside, GIR 0AA; tel. 051 928 8181.
BANKING INFORMATION SERVICE, 10 Lombard Street, London, EC3V 9AR; tel. 01-626 8486.
BARCLAYS BANK plc, 54 Lombard Street, London, EC3; tel. 01-626 1567.
LLOYDS BANK plc, 71 Lombard Street, London, EC3P 3BS; tel. 01-626 1500.
MIDLAND BANK plc, Poultry, London, EC2; tel. 01-606 9911.
NATIONAL WESTMINSTER BANK plc, 41 Lothbury, London, EC2; tel. 01-726 1000.
TSB GROUP, 3 Copthall Avenue, London, EC2P 2AB.
TSB TRUSTCARD, 93/94 Queens Road, Brighton, BN1 3XE.

Travel

Ask for details of cheap travel schemes for young people at travel agents. Some of the possibilities are listed below.

YOUNG PERSON'S RAILCARD, available to people aged 16–23 inclusive, and to students over that age holding a student's card; valid for 12 months from the date of issue, the cards cost £12 and entitle users to a 2nd-class ordinary single or return or Awayday return ticket at half the adult fare price.*

INTER-RAIL SPECIAL YOUTH TRAVEL FACILITY, available to anyone under 26, they cost £115 and allow unlimited travel in 19 different European countries for one month at 50 per cent of the 2nd-class ordinary single or return fare.*

TRANSALPINO LTD offers a 50 per cent reduction to people under 26 on standard rail fares to over 2000 European destinations, with tickets valid for 2 months. En route you can change your route and break your journey as desired. Budget accommodation can also be booked through Transalpino's Hotel Reservations department.

London: 71/75 Buckingham Palace Road, London, SW1; tel. 01-834 9656/6283. Also at kiosk in Victoria Station, Hudsons Place, London, SW1; 214 Shaftesbury Avenue, London, WC2, tel. 01-836 0087/8 and 117 Euston Road, London, NW1, tel. 01-388 2267.

Birmingham: 11 Snow Hill, Queensway, Birmingham; tel. 236 2507/236 7469.

Liverpool: 3 Myrtle Parade, Myrtle Street, Liverpool; tel. 7089 462.

Oxford: Trans World Travel, 19 High Street, Oxford; tel. 726875/6/7.

Edinburgh: 14 North Bridge, Edinburgh; tel. 5573140.

Glasgow: 150 West George Street, Glasgow; tel. 3339177.

Belfast: 24 Lombard Street, Belfast; tel. 248823.

Dublin: 24 Talbot Street, Dublin; tel. 723825.

THE NATIONAL BUS COMPANY offers the cheapest form of long-distance travel both within the UK and to the Continent. Under-17s qualify for the child's fare, which is calculated at two-thirds of the adult fare. Students in full-time education and holding an International Student Identity Card (available from colleges or from the NUS, page 166), are also entitled to the child's rate. National Bus Company, 172 Buckingham Palace Road, London, SW1; tel. 01-730 0202.

EUROWAYS is a Continental coach operator with scheduled

---

* For details of young people's rail fares contact British Railways Board, Rail House, Euston Square, London, NW1 2DZ; tel. 01-262 3232.

services to and from most major European centres, with youth fares for under-25s on selected services.

FERRIES P & O Ferries offer student fares on their cross-Channel routes; tel. 0304 203399.

The Young Person's Railcard mentioned above entitles holders to fare reductions on many Sealink services, e.g. to/from the Isle of Wight (rail/ship only), between Great Britain and Irish ports (rail/ship), to/from/between Channel Islands (rail/ship or ship only), to/from Isle of Man via Heysham (rail/ship).

Various other student fares are available on ferry routes including those to/from Scandinavia (Olau Line) and Belfast (Belfast Car Ferries); ask the operator before booking any ferry trip.

AIR Various youth fares are available from the scheduled airlines; there is a 25 per cent discount off the normal fare to/from Europe. However, there are now so many low-cost travel schemes available to all that it often works out cheaper to buy a normal APEX ticket, or whatever. But if you do not want to be tied down by the strict regulations governing APEX tickets you may be better off with a youth ticket, for which you must produce your passport or birth certificate as proof of date of birth before you can make a reservation.

For travel to the USA there are no special young people's rates. Discounted fares vary according to the individual airline.

CHARTER FLIGHTS Numerous operators offer very cheap air tickets using charter seats; flying 'off-peak', such as in the middle of the night, can bring down prices further still. No reductions are made for students or youth passengers but the prices compare very favourably with scheduled fares.

PACKAGE HOLIDAYS Various tour companies operate and market holidays for specific age groups, especially the young, from children through teenage to 18–30 holidays. Ask for brochures at your travel agent's and watch for advertisements in national newspapers.

YOUTH HOSTELS ASSOCIATION offers inexpensive holidays, mainly for young people but also for families, in Britain and abroad. Write for details to YHA, Trevelyan House, St Albans, Herts.; tel. 0727 55215.

Chapter 7 STAYING HEALTHY and
Chapter 9 SEX MATTERS

Useful addresses
HEALTH EDUCATION COUNCIL, 78 New Oxford Street,

London, WC1A 1AH; tel. 01-637 1881.

BROOK ADVISORY CENTRES, Central Office: 153A East
Street, London, SE17 2SD; tel. 01-708 1234.

Regional centres:

Birmingham: 9 York Road, Birmingham, B16 9HX; tel.
021 455 0491.

City Centre Brook, Top floor, 8–10 Albert Street, Birmingham,
B4 7UD; tel. 021 643 5341.

Handsworth Brook Centre, 102 Hamstead Road,
Handsworth, Birmingham, B19 1DG; tel. 021 554 7553.

Saltley Brook Centre, 3 Washwood Heath Road, Saltley,
Birmingham, B8 1SH; tel. 021 328 4544.

Bristol: Brook Advisory Centre (Avon), 21 Richmond Hill,
Clifton, Bristol, BS8 1BA; tel. 0272 736657.

Coventry: Gynaecological Out-patients, Coventry and
Warwickshire Hospital, Stoney Stanton Road, Coventry; tel.
0203 412627.

Edinburgh: 2 Lower Gilmore Place (office), 50 Gilmore Place
(centre), Edinburgh, EH3 9NY; tel. 031 229 3596.

Merseyside: Brook Look-In, 9 Gambier Terrace, Liverpool, L1
7BG; tel. 051 709 4558.

London: 233 Tottenham Court Road, London, W1P 9AE; tel.
01-323 1522 (enquiries), 01-580 2991 (appointments).

Telephone 01-580 2991 for appointments at:

Shoreditch Brook Centre, 210 Kingsland Road, London, E2
8EB.

Islington Brook Centre, 6–9 Manor Gardens (off Holloway
Road), London, N7 6LA; tel. 01-272 5599.

Brixton Brook Centre, 53 Acre Lane, London, SW2 5TN; tel.
01-274 4995.

Barnsbury Centre, Barnsbury Clinic, Carnegie Street,
London, N1 9QW.

Newham Centre, West Ham Lane Clinic, Stratford, London,
E15 4PT.

Walworth Brook Centre, 153a East Street, Walworth, London,
SE17 2SD; tel. 01-703 9660 or 01-703 7880.

Telephone 01-703 9660 or 01-703 7880 for appointments at:

Stockwell Brook Centre, Rose McAndrew Community Health
Service Clinic, Beale House, Lingham Street, London, SW9.

Lewisham Brook Centre, Lewisham Hospital, Ante-Natal
Dept., Lewisham High Street, London, SE13 6LH.

Kennington Brook Centre, Moffat Health Centre, Sancroft
Street, off Kennington Road, London, SE11 5NG.

Wandsworth Centre, St Christopher's Health Centre,
Wheeler Court, Plough Road, London, SW11 2AY.

FAMILY PLANNING ASSOCIATION (Head Office), 27
Mortimer Street, London, W1A 4QW; tel. 01-636 7866. For local
centres see telephone directory.

THE BLENHEIM PROJECT, an advice centre and counselling
service for drug-users, their friends and families: 7 Thorpe
Close, London, W10 5XL; tel. 01-960 5599. Normally open
weekdays 10 am–5 pm. Telephone first.

408 CONSULTATION CENTRE, advice centre for emotional
and sexual problems including contraception and pregnancy;
for all age groups, male and female. Clinic times vary, so
telephone first. 408 Ecclesall Road, Sheffield, S11 8PJ; tel.
Sheffield 662341.

PREGNANCY ADVISORY SERVICES: look in local telephone
directory.

LIFE – SAVE THE UNBORN CHILD ASSOCIATION (Head
Office), 7 Parade, Leamington Spa, Warwickshire; tel.
0926 21587. Also 250 local groups throughout Britain.

CATHOLIC CHILD WELFARE COUNCIL, 1a Stert Street,
Abingdon, Oxon, OX14 3JF.

NATIONAL COUNCIL FOR ONE-PARENT FAMILIES, 255
Kentish Town Road, London, NW5 2LX; tel. 01-267 1361.

LIFELINE, for anti-abortion advice, 39 Victoria Street, London,
SW1; tel. 01-222 6392. Also regional offices.

ALCOHOLICS ANONYMOUS, 11 Redcliffe Gardens, London,
SW1O 9BQ; tel. 01-352 9779.

NATIONAL COUNCIL ON ALCOHOLISM, Hope House, 45
Great Peter Street, London, SW1P 3LT.

ACTION ON SMOKING, 27–35 Mortimer Street, London,
W1N 7RJ.

THE SAMARITANS, 17 Uxbridge Road, Slough SL1 3UX. See
telephone directory for local contact line.

ALBANY TRUST, for counselling on all sexual matters, 16–18
Strutton Ground, London, SW1P 2HP.

LONDON RAPE CRISIS CENTRE, PO Box 69, London,
WC1X 9NJ; tel. 01-837 1600 (24-hour telephone line). Office line
01-278 3956, weekdays 10 am–6 pm.

LESBIAN LINE, BM Box 1514, London, WC1N 3XX; tel. 01-
837 8602, Monday and Friday 2–10 pm, Tuesday to Thursday
7–10 pm.

LONDON GAY SWITCHBOARD, 24-hour telephone line
01-837 7324.

GRAPEVINE, 296 Holloway Road, London, N7 for sex
education, information and counselling for under-30s.

BRITISH MEDICAL ASSOCIATION, BMA House, Tavistock
Square, London, WC1H 9JP.

VENEREAL DISEASE CLINICS: see local telephone directory or address in public lavatory.
RELEASE, drugs and legal advisory service, 1 Elgin Avenue, London, W9 3PR; tel. 01-289 1123.

Chapter 11 A CHANCE TO LEARN

Useful addresses
ENGLISH TOURIST BOARD, 4 Grosvenor Gardens, London, SW1W 0DU; tel. 01-730 3145.
MANPOWER SERVICES COMMISSION, Regional Information Centre, 166 High Holborn, London, WC1V 6PF; tel. 01-836 1213.
TOPS: see Manpower Services Commission.
NATIONAL INSTITUTE OF ADULT CONTINUING EDUCATION, 19b De Montfort Street, Leicester, LE1 7GE; tel. 0533 551451.
DEPARTMENT OF EDUCATION AND SCIENCE:
England: Room 2/11, Elizabeth House, York Road, London, SE1 7PH.
Wales: Welsh Office, Information Division, Crown Offices, Cathays Park, Cardiff, CF1 3NQ.
Scotland: Scottish Education Dept., New St Andrews House, St James Centre, Edinburgh, EH1 3SX.
Regional offices:
London and Home Counties: Regional Advisory Council for Technological Education, Tavistock House South, Tavistock Square, London, WC1H 9LR; tel. 01-388 0027.
East Anglia: Regional Advisory Council for Further Education, Shire Hall, Bury St Edmunds, Suffolk, IP33 2AN; tel. 0284 63141.
East Midlands: East Midlands Further Education Council, Robins Wood House, Robins Wood Road, Aspley, Nottingham, NG8 3NH; tel. 0602 293291.
North: Council for Further Education, 5 Grosvenor Villas, Grosvenor Road, Newcastle-on-Tyne, NE2 2RU; tel. 0632 813242/3.
North West: Regional Advisory Council for Further Education, The Town Hall, Walkden Road, Worsley, Manchester, M28 4QE; tel. 061 702 8700.
South: Regional Council for Further Education, 26 Bath Road, Reading, RG1 6NT; tel. 0734 52120.
South West: Regional Council for Further Education, Wessex Lodge, 11/13 Billetfield, Taunton, Somerset, TA1 1HR; tel. 0823 85491.

West Midlands: West Midlands Advisory Council for Further Education, Norfolk House, Smallbrook, Queensway, Birmingham, B5 4NB; tel. 021 643 8924.
Yorkshire and Humberside: Council for Further Education, Bowling Green Terrace, Jack Lane, Leeds, LS11 9SX; tel. 0532 40751.
DEPARTMENT OF EDUCATION (NORTHERN IRELAND), Rathgael House, Balloo Road, Bangor, Co. Down, BR19 2PR.
BUSINESS AND TECHNICIAN EDUCATION COUNCIL, Central House, Upper Woburn Place, London, WC1H 0HH.
ROYAL SOCIETY OF ART Examinations Board, John Adam Street, London, WC2N 6EZ.
CAREERS AND OCCUPATIONAL INFORMATION CENTRE (COIC), Room W1101, Moor Foot, Sheffield, S1 4PQ.
CITY AND GUILDS OF LONDON INSTITUTE, 76 Portland Place, London, W1N 4AA; tel. 01-580 3050.
NATIONAL EXTENSION COLLEGE, 18 Brooklands Avenue, Cambridge, CB2 2HN; tel. 0223 316644.
OPEN UNIVERSITY, for guide to BA degree courses, PO Box 48, Milton Keynes, MK7 6AB; tel. 0908 79685/6; for guide to Associate Student Programme, PO Box 76, Milton Keynes, MK7 6AN.
UNIVERSITIES CENTRAL COUNCIL FOR ADMISSIONS (UCCA), PO Box 28, Cheltenham, Glos, GL50 1HY.
FAMILY WELFARE ASSOCIATION, 501 Kingsland Road, London, E8 4AU.
NATIONAL UNION OF STUDENTS, 461 Holloway Road, London, N7 6LJ; tel. 01-272 8900.
ACE ADVISORY CENTRE FOR EDUCATION, 18 Victoria Park Square, Bethnal Green, London, E2 9PB; tel. 01-980 4596.

Chapter 12 TIME TO SPARE

Useful addresses
THE LADY, 39–40 Bedford Street, Strand, London, WC2; tel. 01-836 8705.
COMMUNITY SERVICE VOLUNTEERS (CSV), 237 Pentonville Road, London, N1 9NJ; tel. 01-278 6601.
VOLUNTARY SERVICE OVERSEAS (VSO), 9 Belgrave Square, London, SW1; tel. 01-235 5191.
WORLD COMMUNITY DEVELOPMENT SERVICE, 27 Montagu Road, Notley, Oxford, OX2 9AH.
PROJECT TRUST, Breacachadh Castle, Isle of Coll, Argyll.

Reference section

CENTRAL BUREAU FOR EDUCATIONAL VISITS AND
EXCHANGES, Seymour Mews House, Seymour Mews,
London, W1H 9DE.
INTERNATIONAL VOLUNTARY SERVICE, Ceresole House,
53 Regent Road, Leicester, LE1 6YL.
CAREERS RESEARCH AND ADVISORY CENTRE (CRAC),
Bateman Street, Cambridge, CB2 1LZ.
CHRISTIANS ABROAD, 15 Tufton Street, London, SW1P 3QQ;
tel. 01-222 2165.
GAP ACTIVITY PROJECTS LTD, 2 South Drive, Leighton Park
School, Reading, Berks, RG2 7DP.
MACDONALD & EVANS LTD, Estover Road, Plymouth,
PL6 7PZ.
THE VOLUNTEER CENTRE, 29 Lower King's Road,
Berkhamsted, Herts, HP4 2AB; tel. 04427 73311.
NATIONAL COUNCIL FOR VOLUNTARY
ORGANIZATIONS, 26 Bedford Square, London, WC1B 3HU.
NATIONAL YOUTH BUREAU, 17–23 Albion Street, Leicester,
LE1 6GD.
BRITISH TRUST FOR CONSERVATION VOLUNTEERS, 36 St
Mary's Street, Wallingford, Oxon, OX10 0EU; tel. 0491 39766.
Regional offices:
Scotland: Scottish Conservation Projects Trust, 70 Main Street,
Doune, Perthshire, FK16 6BW; tel. 0786 841479.
North East: 423 Chillingham Road, Heaton, Newcastle-upon-
Tyne, NE6 5QU; tel. 0632 651820.
North West: 40 Cannon Street, Preston, Lancs, PR1 3NT; tel.
0772 50286.
West and North Yorkshire: Hollybush Farm, Broad Lane,
Kirkstall, Leeds, Yorks; tel. 0532 742335.
South Yorkshire: Conservation Volunteers Training Centre,
Balby Road, Balby, Doncaster, DH4 0RH; tel. 0302 859522.
East Midlands: Conservation Volunteers Training Centre,
United Reform Church, Gregory Boulevard, Nottingham; tel.
0602 705493/705539.
West Midlands: 577 Bristol Road, Selly Oak, Birmingham 29; tel.
021 471 2558.
Wales: Forest Farm, Forest Farm Road, Whitchurch, Cardiff; tel.
0222 626660.
East Anglia: Bayfordbury House, Hertford, Herts, SG13 8LO;
tel. 0992 53067.
Thames and Chilterns: 36 St Mary's Street, Wallingford, Oxon,
OX10 0EU; tel. 0491 39766.
South West: The Old Estate Yard, Newton St Loe, Bath, Avon;
tel. 02217 2856.

London: 2 Mandela Street (formerly Upper Selous Street),
Camden Town, London, NW1; tel. 01-388 3946.
South: Hatchlands, East Clandon, Guildford, Surrey, GU4 7RT;
tel. 0483 223294.
Northern Ireland: The Pavilion, Cherryvale Park, Ravenhill
Road, Belfast, BT6 0BZ; tel. 0232 645169.
WINGED FELLOWSHIP TRUST, 58 College Road, London
SE21.
PENSIONERS' LINK, 17 Balfe Street, London, N1 9EB.
VACATION WORK, 9 Park End Street, Oxford.
COUNCIL FOR VOLUNTARY ACTION, for information about
voluntary organizations in Wales, Crescent Road, Caerphilly,
Mid Glamorgan; tel. 0222 869224.
SCOTTISH COUNCIL OF SOCIAL SERVICE, for information
about voluntary organizations in Scotland, 18–19 Claremont
Crescent, Edinburgh; tel. 031 556 3883.
NORTHERN IRELAND COUNCIL OF SOCIAL SERVICE, for
information about voluntary organizations in Northern Ireland,
2 Annandale Road, Belfast, N. Ireland; tel. 0232 640011.
DUKE OF EDINBURGH AWARD OFFICE, 5 Prince of Wales
Terrace, Kensington, London, W8 5PG; tel. 01-937 5205.
Regional offices:
Scotland: 69 Dublin Street, Edinburgh, EH3 6NS; tel.
031 556 9097.
Wales: 17 Cathedral Road, Cardiff, CF1 9HA; tel. 0222 28570.
Northern Ireland: 593 Lisburn Road, Belfast, BT9 7GS; tel.
0232 667123.
England:
North East: c/o Richardsons Westgarth and Co Ltd, Wallsend,
Tyne & Wear, NE28 6QL; tel. 0632 625306.
North West: 4 Bolton Street, Ramsbottom, Bury, Lancashire,
BL0 9HX; tel. 070 682 4821.
Midlands: 182 Soho Hill, Birmingham, B19 1AG; tel.
021 523 3891.
East: The Community Centre, London Road, Stony Stratford,
Milton Keynes, Bucks, MK11 1JA; tel. 0908 566652.
South East: 35 Elm Road, New Malden, Surrey, KT3 3HB; tel.
01-949 2777.
South West: 9–13 Bath Street, Bath, BA1 1SA; tel. 0225 64141.
ROYAL JUBILEE TRUSTS, 8 Buckingham Street, London,
WC2N 6BU.
Scotland: Scottish Committee of the Royal Jubilee Trusts, 15
Moredum Park Court, Edinburgh.
Wales: Welsh Committee of The Royal Jubilee Trusts, Council
for Wales of Voluntary Youth Services, 2 Washington

Chambers, Stanwell Road, Penarth, South Glamorgan.
Northern Ireland: Northern Ireland Committee of the Royal
Jubilee Trusts, Standing Conference of Youth Organizations, 50
University Street, Belfast, BT7 1HB.

Chapter 13 IF YOU ARE DISABLED

Useful addresses
NATIONAL BUREAU FOR HANDICAPPED STUDENTS, 40
Brunswick Square, London, SW1; tel. 01-278 3459.
ACTION RESEARCH FOR THE CRIPPLED CHILD, Vincent
House, North Parade, Horsham, West Sussex, RH12 2DA.
VOLUNTARY COUNCIL FOR HANDICAPPED CHILDREN,
c/o National Children's Bureau, 8 Wakeley Street, London, EC1;
tel. 01-278 9441.
MENCAP, 123 Golden Lane, London, EC1Y 0RT; tel. 01-253
9433.
ROYAL NATIONAL INSTITUTE FOR THE BLIND, 224 Great
Portland Street, London, W1N 6AA; tel. 01-388 1266.
NATIONAL DEAF CHILDREN'S SOCIETY, 45 Hereford Road,
London, W2; tel 01-229 9272/3/4/5.
GATEWAY CLUBS, MENCAP, 123 Golden Lane, London,
EC1Y 0RT; tel. 01-253 9433.
THE SPORTS COUNCIL, 16 Upper Woburn Place, London,
WC1H 0QP; tel. 01-388 1277.
BRITISH SPORTS ASSOCIATION FOR THE DISABLED,
Hayward House, Harvey Road, Aylesbury, Bucks, HP21 8PP;
tel. Aylesbury 27889.
DISABLED LIVING FOUNDATION, 380/384 Harrow Road,
London, W9 2HV; tel. 01-289 6111.
ROYAL NATIONAL INSTITUTE FOR THE DEAF, 105 Gower
Street, London, WC1E 6AH; tel. 01-387 8033. Also 9a Clairmont
Gardens, Glasgow, G3 7LW; tel. 041 332 0343.
ROYAL ASSOCIATION FOR DISABILITY AND
REHABILITATION (RADAR), 25 Mortimer Street, London,
W1N 8AB; tel. 01-637 5400.
ASSOCIATION FOR THE SEXUAL AND PERSONAL
RELATIONSHIPS OF THE DISABLED (SPOD), The Diorama,
14 Peto Place, London, NW1 4DT; tel. 01-486 9823/4.
GEMMA, BM Box 5700, London, WC1N 3XX.

Chapter 15 YOU, THE CITIZEN

Useful addresses
NATIONAL ASSOCIATION OF CITIZENS' ADVICE
BUREAUX, Myddleton House, 115/123 Pentonville Road,
London, N1. (For local offices see telephone directory.)
WOMEN'S NATIONAL COMMISSION, Government Offices,
Great George Street, London, SW1P 3AQ; tel. 01-233 4208.
RIGHTS OF WOMEN, 374 Grays Inn Road, London, WC1; tel.
01-278 6349.
EQUAL OPPORTUNITIES COMMISSION, Overseas House,
Quay Street, Manchester, M3 3HN; tel. 061 833 9244.
CONSUMERS' ASSOCIATION, 14 Buckingham Street,
London, WC2N 6DS; tel. 01-839 1222.
OFFICE OF FAIR TRADING, Field House, Breams Buildings,
London, EC4; tel. 01-242 2858.
NATIONAL CONSUMER COUNCIL, 18 Queen Anne's Gate,
London, SW1; tel. 01-222 9501.
ELECTRICITY CONSUMERS' COUNCIL, Brook House, 2/16
Torrington Place, London, WC1E 7II; tel. 01-636 5703.
CHILD POVERTY ACTION GROUP, 1 Macklin Street, London,
WC2; tel. 01-242 3225.
THE LAW SOCIETY, 113 Chancery Lane, London, WC2A 1PL;
tel. 01-242 1222.
LAW CENTRES FEDERATION, 164 North Gower Street,
London, NW1 2ND and local centres.
HOME OFFICE, 50 Queen Anne's Gate, London, SW1H 9AT;
tel. 01-213 3030.
NATIONAL COUNCIL FOR CIVIL LIBERTIES, 21 Tabard
Street, London, SE1 4LA; tel. 01-403 3888.
COMMISSION FOR RACIAL EQUALITY, 10–12 Allington
Street, London, SW1; tel. 01-828 7022.
INSURANCE OMBUDSMAN BUREAU, 31 Southampton Row,
London, WC1; tel. 01-404 0591.
RELEASE, for advice on drug problems, 1 Elgin Avenue,
London, W9 3PR; tel. 01-289 1123.
REGISTRATION OF BIRTHS, DEATHS AND MARRIAGES, St
Catherine's House, 10 Kingsway, London, WC2; tel. 01-
242 0262.
RAPE CRISIS CENTRE (LONDON); tel. 01-837 1600.

Index